:1

I hope the
Stories told
on these Pages
inspire you to
keep going when
you feel like
giving up.

Davi Bro

Acts 14:22

Galatians 6:9

CROOKED RIVER STORIES

A Memoir Of Perseverance

DARIN BROWN

© Darin Brown 2020

ISBN: 978-1-09834-358-3

eBook ISBN: 978-1-09834-359-0

To mom and dad

Your crooked river lives combined into a single stream which not only brought me into the world but resulted in every word in this book. I love you dearly.

PROLOGUE

D own from its headwaters in the Ozark Mountains, through the gently sloping fields, farms, and forests of rural Missouri, up to its union with the Missouri River, the waters of the Gasconade River meander along a path that is crooked and calm. Through its confluence with the Missouri, these waters eventually join the Mississippi, that great American artery which Mark Twain described as "well worth reading about," a river "in all ways remarkable." Hardly anyone has heard of the Gasconade River, but more people should know about it.

The Gasconade River was named by French fur traders for Native Americans who fished the river and hunted game on its banks. The name literally means "extravagant boasting" but today there is really not much intrigue or even interest in this humble river. A Google search of the Gasconade will yield state park data, real estate listings, highway bridge repairs, and an article on the Gasconade bridge train disaster, and pretty much none of the beauty or mystery that makes this remarkable river every bit as worthy as its more famous main stem rivers.

But to those of us who have actually floated, fished, and swam in its waters there is an entirely different story to tell.

In his book, *The Rivers of Missouri,* author Dru Pippin describes the Gasconade's many small beauties:

"...steep bluffs, gorgeous cuts, hairpin turns and lazy eddies, hardwoods, softwoods, and dogwoods, hidden logs, protruding boulders that weathering has tumbled down adjacent cliffs, wildflowers and shrubs, birds and bees, four legged creatures quenching their thirst at my water's edge while listless white clouds float above as though convoying my trip."

Pippin's description takes me back to the river of my youth and the countless times I floated and fished it with my dad and brothers.

I can close my eyes and still smell the Gasconade. Its aroma is a stew of water, rocks, willow grass, moss, and oak trees and yes...even a hint of fish. The very memory of this smell still nourishes my soul.

I can still see my dad sitting on the back bench of our 12-foot aluminum boat. Behind him is a faded blue, 3 horse Evinrude outboard motor which never started on the first pull and sometimes never started at all.

I see the last bit of mist ascending into the air as we paddle early in the morning through the green, milky water to our favorite fishing holes. I see metal clasp stringers on the side of the boat filled with bass, perch, and our favorite fish, goggle eye (rock bass).

I can still feel the sting and tightness of sunburn on my back and the absolute terror I felt every time we saw a snake in the water no matter how far away it was or the countless assurances it was not venomous or going to get in the boat with us. Long before Harrison Ford said it in *Raiders of the Lost Ark*, I hated snakes.

I can still smell, see, and feel the days spent catching fish and the bait used to lure them on the Gasconade. When our fishing lures weren't working, we would try to catch live bait which, to a small boy, is almost as fun as fishing. We had two methods of catching crawdads. The most efficient was to use a window screen stretched out about three feet and attached to two poles. We would get out of the boat on a gravel bar and then, while one person held the screen, the others would walk and kick up submerged rocks steering the crawdads downstream into the screen. Within a few sweeps we would have enough crawdads for fishing. The slower method involved using a plastic drinking cup or cut down soda can. Crawdads move backwards when threatened, so after locating a crawdad we would place the cup or can behind it and use our free hand to scare the crawdad into our cup or can. We would also catch minnows in swift and shallow water using a glass, half gallon sized trap. My dad would crumble saltine crackers into the trap and then carefully place it on the bottom of the river. Within minutes the trap would be teeming with minnows which were lured by the cracker crumbs. They swam through a narrow hole in the glass jar, but for some reason could not or would not swim back out. I still laugh today remembering how my dad would always scold us to stop eating all the crackers or we wouldn't have any left to catch minnows. When fishing for larger fish, which refuse to bite artificial lures, we would clean out an old coffee can and use it to collect large, squirming night crawlers (worms). Just a few digs of the pitchfork into the black Crooked River mud almost always yielded three or four night crawlers which we were more than happy to retrieve and drop into the coffee can along with some clumps of dirt to keep them wet and lively for the end of our hooks.

Around noon on our all-day fishing float trips we would dry dock on a gravel bar and take a lunch break. I can still taste the cold RC cola we kept cold in a green army cooler, along with those cheese and cracker snacks in packets with the little red plastic knife, and the salty Vienna Sausages we had for lunch. Food always tasted better on the river.

These memories are now over thirty years and a thousand miles away, but they shaped me in powerful ways.

These memories of the Gasconade River's beauty are byproducts of its persistence. You see, the Gasconade River is one of those unusual rivers that runs from south to north. Over 300 miles and seven counties in south central Missouri, the Gasconade meanders and cuts through the hard dirt, sandstone and bedrock of the Ozark Salem Plateau in what, from a map's perspective, looks like an uphill trajectory.

Scientists tell us we shouldn't be impressed with rivers running north. Water, they tell us, always follows the path of least resistance but the Gasconade's crooked trajectory tells a story of perseverance we all need to hear. The river's identity and purpose can only be found in its struggle to reach its destiny. Near my birth city, Waynesville Missouri, there is an area where you can float the Gasconade for 15 miles or walk for two miles. I guess by now you know which way I'm going with those options.

Give me the river! It may be harder and take longer, but the memories will be greater and the beauty will last longer.

My dad and I would take day long fishing float trips on the river which covered only 15-20 minutes by car. No wonder the Gasconade River has been called, "one of the crookedest rivers in the world." (Southwestpaddler.com 8/17/12)

The Gasconade River aptly fits the quote attributed to James Watkins.

"A river cuts through rock, not because of its power, but because of its persistence."

The Gasconade refuses to give up.

Other than knowing God's love for me, there is no other lesson in my life I have needed to learn and apply more often than the lesson to keep going and not give up. The need to persevere through life's challenges comes up again and again and again in my life and probably yours as well. Much of what I have learned in this area has been caught rather than taught. The classrooms that best showed me the value of not quitting have been stories and experiences.

That's what this book is. It is a collection of the stories from my life and the people I have bumped into which have taught me, and continue to teach me, not to give up.

After almost 300 miles of winding and cutting through bedrock on its crooked journey, the Gasconade River which I'll be calling "The Crooked River" finally reaches its end and flows into the Missouri River near a small town which bears its name. The Missouri River, in turn, empties into the Mississippi River which flows all the way to the Gulf of Mexico. Perseverance is the same. It first flows to us and then it flows through us into the lives of others for miles and generations to come.

CHAPTER ONE:
POOR AS A WHIPPOORWILL

God will bless you people who are poor. His kingdom belongs to you.
-Jesus in Luke 6:20

The people who grew up near the Crooked River were as stubborn, determined, and persistent as the river itself. And they were very poor.

This poverty tagged them with belittling epithets like "hicks" and "hillbillies," but it also earned them the label "tough as nails." Despite their impoverished circumstances, these dirt-poor folks somehow kept their resolve and sense of humor. Together, they coined some hilarious and descriptive phrases, like:

"Slicker than snot on a doorknob."

"Slower than molasses in January."

"Nervous as a long-tailed cat in a room full of rocking chairs."

"Dumber than a box of rocks."

And my personal favorite,

"Busier than a cat burying poop."

And finally, one of the Hillbilly expressions which describes several generations of my family and my own upbringing: "poor as a Whippoorwill."

Nothing in my vast study of ornithology led me to any logical reason why Whippoorwills would be any more financially challenged than other birds, so I'm left to my own imagination. Was it poor investments in the birdhouse real estate market? Too many long nights gambling at the cock fights? Or maybe they developed a bad habit of hitting the snooze button in the morning, thus allowing other "early birds to get the worms." Perhaps I'll never know.

My dad, Benny Brown, was born in 1937 in a small farmhouse back when babies were delivered at home. He grew up near a small town called Crocker Missouri and lived about three miles from the Crooked River. His family (mom, dad and older sister) didn't have electricity in the house until he was 12 years old. They added indoor plumbing (not including a bath or toilet) when he turned 16.

The family lived off the land. They cultivated a garden, picked wild berries in the summer and canned everything they could in mason jars. They got drinking water from a nearby spring where they also cooled the milk they got from their cows.

They collected rainwater in a cistern which flowed down a gutter from the rooftop and drained through a box filled with charcoal and gravel. A bucket in the cistern was used to draw water for cooking and cleaning. My grandma used a wash tub and a wooden rub board to scrub clothes on. She used a hand turned rolling device to squeeze out the excess water before hanging the clothes on a clothesline between two trees.

The family occasionally got to eat chicken, but more often than not they ate squirrel in the fall, rabbit in the winter, and fish caught from the Crooked River in the summer. Once a year, they butchered a hog. All their meals were cooked on top of a wood burning stove which also heated the house. Nothing was wasted.

A typical day for my dad included slopping the hogs, checking the chicken coop for eggs, milking the cows and gathering wood for the cook stove. To gain extra money for the family, he would rummage through junk piles and search dirt road ditches for scrap aluminum and steel which were in short supply during World War II.

At the end of the day, my dad would kneel beside a metal water basin and take a sponge bath or, during warm weather months, grab some soap and ride his horse to take a bath in the Crooked River.

At night, the family would gather around an old radio powered by a huge battery and listen to programs like *The Lone Ranger*, *Amos and Andy*, and *The Durango Kid*.

On Saturdays, the family would hook a horse up to a wagon and head to town where they would purchase essential items they could not produce on their own: things like sugar, coffee, flour, and other dry goods and daily essentials. Even the poor were subject to rationing practices during WWII, so the family received coupons or tickets which limited the quantity of certain items they could purchase.

My dad's favorite Christmas memory was the year his sister, Gladys, the most beautiful girl in Pulaski County, received a 5-cent bottle of finger-nail polish. My dad received a toy pistol made of sawdust that morning, he broke it by Christmas dinner.

When my dad turned ten, the family was finally able to purchase their first car which made several trips to and from Washington and Oregon so the family could work in canneries during the pea harvest season during tough financial times. They made just enough money to get back home and survive for a few more months.

Life was incredibly hard and fragile growing up poor near the Crooked River. Without access to medicine and doctors, people didn't live as long or get the crucial care that others living in or closer to bigger towns received. When someone got sick, family members and neighbors would take shifts through the night and sit beside the bed of the afflicted, dabbing their head with cool wash cloths and praying they would make it through the night.

However, life on the Crooked River does not only yield crooked fortune. Eventually, my dad fell in love with a Crooked River girl from

Waynesville, named Judy Hearst. She was middle class, which meant she grew up with indoor plumbing, including a toilet and bathtub. The greatest obstacle to their relationship came on the day she was to meet the Hillbilly parents. Surrounded by farm animals, chickens, dogs, cats and swarms of flies, my mom persevered to find love. She passed the true test of love when she successfully used an outhouse for the very first time! This is likely not what the J. Geils Band had in mind when they sang "Love Stinks. They were married December 24th, 1959.

Breaking the chain of generational poverty is never easy. With no high school diploma and very few job opportunities my dad began married life unemployed while my mom brought home $4 a day working at a dry cleaner. Eventually, as they prepared for a family, dad got a couple driving jobs: one as a bus shuttle driver for soldiers based at Fort Leonard Wood and another as dump truck driver for a construction company. Neither of these jobs provided a steady income, though, so he had to seek more reliable pay elsewhere. This led him to his employment at a tire shop in Dixon, a small town about ten miles from Crocker. At the tire shop, he did more than just fix flats and install new tires. The shop he worked for recapped old tires through a rigorous retreading process. My dad and his coworkers would lathe the rough spots off the tires on a spinning mechanical wheel, wrap sheets of heavy rubber around the buffed tires, and, finally, place the wrapped tires in burning hot molds. It was a backbreaking, hot, and dirty job. The old and bald tires would come in and then leave the shop clean and renewed, and my father would leave covered in the sweat and debris of a hard day's work. Some kids associate their father's love with how many toys their dads gave them or how many trips they took them on, but I have always associated my dad's love for me with the tiny, black rubber chips embedded in his forearm hair as we gathered around the family dinner table every night at the exact same time. His hard work for our family was how I knew I was loved.

Dad toiled at the tire shop for $65 a week while providing for a family of five. After 15 years, he got bumped up to $100 a week. I am still not sure how our family survived.

When my youngest brother's birth made us a family of six, my dad left the tire shop and got a much better paying job working as a butcher for the local grocery store. When my youngest brother started school, my mom retired with honors from being a stay at home working mom to working in the cafeteria at our school. We were inching our way closer to the poverty line.

Growing up poor meant we ate a lot of beans and cornbread—often a couple times a week—but we hardly ever complained. Like my dad's family, we grew fond of rabbit. Every year we would make two or three trips to Mennonite farms in north central Missouri and ask the farmers if we could hunt on their land. They always kindly allowed us to hunt, and we always killed lots of rabbits there. Upon returning home, we would clean the rabbits and, believe it or not, throw them in the bathtub where they would soak before my mom, with surgical precision, would go over each rabbit, ensuring not a single piece of fur or buckshot was on or embedded in the rabbit before freezing it. There are some childhood memories you simply can't get out of your head no matter how hard you try, and dozens of naked rabbit bodies floating in pink water in your bathtub is one of them.

As a sign of upward financial mobility, our family ate way less squirrel than my dad's family. It wasn't so much for a lack of squirrel hunting opportunities as it was my mom's displeasure for their gamey taste. I tended to agree. Like my dad's family, we ate fish and frog legs from the Crooked River. We had a small garden filled with green beans, cucumbers and strawberries. We also had tomato plants which grew alongside of our barn. We occasionally ate wild mushrooms and quail. Unlike my dad's family, we were able to have venison (the deer population in Missouri for years was virtually nonexistent) and instead of butchering a hog we sent one of the few cows we had on our small acre farm to the butcher.

My mom, it was said, could not even boil water when she married my dad. However, she became a master chef in our eyes and was somehow always able to provide delicious food for four hungry children and her husband even if that meant waiting for everyone to devour their food first before she would dig into what was left over. This was especially true of fried chicken, which inspired a form of an ancient Caste System which ruled in our home. Dad and my oldest brother Troy always got the big white pieces of chicken while my younger brother Landis, my younger sister, Kristan and I gobbled up legs and thighs. This system left my mom with the back and some tiny wings or other unidentified pieces. She never complained.

We got our milk from a farmer who brought it to our house in big glass jars and I can remember stirring off the cream which rose to the top. We got our eggs from another farmer my mom simply called the "egg man."

One day, the egg man brought live chickens. I asked my mom if we were going to keep them. She said, "Yes, but only for a day." I knew this was bad news for the chickens, yet I recognized that I would finally get to realize one of my childhood dreams and actually witness the phenomenon known as "running around like a chicken with its head cut off." To my animal loving friends: please know we were simply providing food for our family, and swift decapitation with a hatchet is the most humane way to send a chicken to Glory. And for the record, no chickens were harmed in the retelling of this story.

I'll spare you the details, but the old Hillbilly expression "running around like a chicken with your head cut off" is true. I saw it happen with my own two eyes. They do, in fact, run around a bit after their soul has gone to the big chicken coop in the sky. Some lasted longer than others and some refused to do anything at all, but much like the rabbits in the bathtub, some childhood memories last forever, and seeing chickens run around with their heads cut off is another memory which is hard to escape from.

After the testosterone driven and adolescent joy of watching chickens run around with their heads cut off, I was ready to move on to something new, like playing basketball. Mom and dad had a different plan. For the next several hours we plucked and then dunked chicken carcasses in hot water only to bring them out and pluck them some more. I was seriously contemplating putting my own head on the chopping block. The only thing that kept me going was the thought that with this many chickens I might be able to break through the Brown family Caste System and actually enjoy the taste of white meat chicken for the first time. Heck, with all these chickens my mom might even be able to get a leg! Then I was informed these chickens which we were plucking in a poorly ventilated shed were not fryers but rather old hens which would be deboned and only used in chicken and dumplings. I hated chicken and dumplings.

There were two houses I remember growing up in. The first one we simply called the yellow house and the second one was the two-story house. At the yellow house, my older brother, younger sister, and I all shared the same room. My sister Kristan, who got all the looks AND the brains in the family, would get to choose who she wanted to sleep with. My brother Troy, on the top bunk, would always point his finger down to my bottom bunk in an effort to get her to sleep with me; at the same time I would be pointing my finger up trying to convince her to choose to sleep with Troy. I'm happy to report that counseling and Christian forgiveness have helped Kristan overcome the torture of living with two, and later, three brothers.

The addition of the third brother, Landis, created the need to move from the yellow house to the two-story house. The two-story house we moved into was one hundred years old and had never been insulated, which meant it was freezing cold in the winter and boiling hot in the summer. Because we couldn't afford a gas furnace, we tried to warm the entire house with a wood burning stove. The stove burned up a lot of wood but only heated a space in our house the size of a dish towel, which also happened to be a space no one ever actually occupied. The heat had no chance to make it to the upstairs bedrooms where we could have easily filmed an episode of *Life Below Zero*. To protect myself from hypothermia I had to sleep with my two brothers. My older brother took up about 95% of the bed, leaving me and my younger brother sleeping on the outer edge. My younger brother would not sleep unless he had a handful of hair from the back of my head. To this day I still have a patch of hair that won't lay straight. It was not uncommon for us to wake up in the morning and find icicles hanging from the pant legs of wet jeans my mom had hung on the wrought iron banister that protected us from falling down the stairs. Our water pipes would always freeze up, requiring hair dryers and frantic efforts of pouring hot water at the source of where they froze. Some nights were so cold my dad and I took shifts adding wood to the fire to keep people and pipes from freezing.

In the summer, it was suffocating. We had one box fan for the entire house. My parents kept it in their room and faced it outside their bedroom window. They tried to convince us that using the fan in exhaust mode would suck all the hot air out of the entire house while allowing cool summer breezes to pour through our windows. They assured us this would even be true in our upstairs bedrooms. I never really bought into the science behind their explanation but there was no arguing and no alternatives, so I would go downstairs to our only bathroom, wet a wash-cloth, place it on my head and wish for daylight. More times than I can remember I would wake up in a hot sweat having dreamed about chickens...and dumplings.

One of the most humiliating things about growing up poor, at least for me, was having to wear hand- me- down clothes. I probably would have been OK wearing my older brother's clothes, which was a pretty common practice among Crooked River people, but it never happened. My brother, Troy, was big boned, muscular, and had a barrel chest. I, on the other hand was a skinny rat with a chicken chest who didn't weigh 100 pounds until after high school. This meant I would be wearing hand me downs from cousins and people we knew from church. If I were president, I would sign an executive order declaring that all hand me downs must be sent to a different city than their origin. If such an order didn't work, then I would write a different one requiring all hand me downs be stored at least three years before they could be worn by others. I would do it for the poor children of America. Neither such law existed to bene-fit me at a crucial time of my social development. Nothing plummets the fragile self-esteem of a young boy more than wearing the same pants to church his cousin or friend wore only a few weeks before and to be greeted with, "Nice pants, where did you get those?" What made it worse was the person asking the question was so often a GIRL!

Even more humiliating to me, though was a piece of mail that my family received when I was 11 years old, a missive that felt so dismis-sive that, at the time, I had wished it were my draft notice to fight in the war instead. As she unfolded the letter, my mom happily announced, "We made it this year." "Made what?" I asked indifferently. "We qualified for free lunches this year," she answered excitedly. To be honest I don't remember all the events that followed the dreaded announcement but I faintly remember my older brother offering to take a 40 hours-a-week job working on the railroad while I vowed to never again leave my bedroom lights on when I came downstairs. But alas, it was too late. We had become "free lunch people." It was an official designation which would alert the world that we were "dirt poor". Alone that night, I lay in my bed devastated by the sudden upheaval in my, up-until-now normal life. As tears ran down my cheeks, I wondered and worried how my friends would stigmatize me for being on the free lunch program.

The school bell seemed to ring louder as I took my place in a desk which almost swallowed me in my new sixth grade classroom on that hot and humid late August Monday. It was the first day of school. Each school day begin with roll call combined with lunch purchase intentions. In my mind, roll/lunch call was a cleverly devised communist plot which neatly divided the economic conditions of every family who lived near the Crooked River. The economic class distinctions are still vivid in my mind.

First, there were the kids who, when their names were called, proudly barked, "I brought my lunch." These were the upper class. Their parents sent them to school with the latest designer lunch boxes packed with expensive deli meat sandwiches cut into perfect triangles, pre-packaged potato chips, thermoses filled with chocolate milk and some other expensive snack cake like Twinkies or Ho Hos.

Second came the kids who, when called, smiled like opossums and called out, "Paid" when their names were called. These were the members of the upper middle-class, whose parents had forgotten just how bad school lunches were and paid on their kid's account a week or a month in advance.

Next came the group of which I had been a member in previous years, a class which combined the middle and lower classes. When their names were called, they cried out, almost victoriously, "Charge!" and then laughed. Their parents lived on the financial edge and would wait until they received death threats from the school for late fees before finally scraping enough money together to pay as much as they could. The members of this lower-middle class always had lingering balances even into the summer months.

Finally, there was the group that could call me its newest member. The pathetic lower class also known as free lunch people. We were at the bottom rung of the proverbial ladder of success and were required to announce it to the world when our names were called, and we were required to announce it every single day. When our names were called, we were to simply say, "Free." We might as well have announced ourselves like lepers of old: "Unclean, unclean."

And so it was on the first day of sixth grade. I sat in my desk, hoping it would actually swallow me, awaiting my fate and dreading the subsequent shame which would surely come as my entire sixth grade class learned I was as poor as a whippoorwill. As our teacher opened her book and began to call names, I wondered why God had invented free lunches and why it was I who had to have them. I also wondered why my mom wouldn't let my brother take the railroad job. And then it began.

"Cecil Adams." He responded, "I brought my lunch." My tiny hands began to sweat.

"John Balston." He proudly barked, "Brought my lunch." My throat began to tighten and close.

"Jennifer Beckett." She replied, "Paid." My pulse quickened. My body tensed.

"Carol Brewer." She answered with a quick "Charge."

Then came my "Oh crap moment." I was next and I would be the first to say, "Free."

"Darin Brown." My mouth opened but nothing audible came out. The teacher softly said "Paid," and then quickly went to the next name.

The gray cloud that hovered over my head had been removed. I thought, "There must be some mistake," but the joy which filled my tiny sixth grade body was greater than the desire for truth and justice. "I'll let it slide this time" I whispered to myself.

The next day I was in the pressure cooker again, and much to my delight, the teacher made the same mistake again. After several weeks of this I finally realized what was happening. My gentle and kind teacher was simply covering up the shame of a free lunch boy. She was always my favorite teacher.

I remember when I was a teenager trying to sleep in my upstairs bedroom on one of those hot summer nights and a whippoorwill landed on the roof separating the two floors of our house. Across the room and right next to the window she began her song. I laid as still as I possibly could as she sang me to sleep with her beautiful melody. She came back the next night and again the next. By night four I was starting to get annoyed and her song sounded more like a mockingbird reminding me I was poor. By night five I was wondering what fried whippoorwill might taste like and how fast I could get to my shotgun.

I write these words today less than twenty-five miles from Washington, DC. I live in one of the richest counties in America, and I'm pretty sure there's a zero percent chance that a whippoorwill will visit my home to sing to me. And yet I can still hear the whippoorwill's song; I welcome the delicate melody every time the winds of memory bring her back to my ear. The song reminds me of my parents, who never once argued about money, but instead believed that God would somehow provide. The song reminds me that He always did, and always does. The song reminds me to be content with what I have, and to pause every day and be thankful. I can still hear the song of the whippoorwill, and it reminds me how I was actually happier when I was poor, and that I was never as rich as I was when I was loved by other poor people who lived by the Crooked River.

CHAPTER TWO:

FALLING OFF A CLIFF AND OTHER NEAR-DEATH EXPERIENCES

Life is pain, Highness. Anyone who says differently is selling something.
-Dread Pirate Roberts, aka Westley, *Princess Bride*, 1987

There's one in every family. A kid who spends every summer in a sling or a cast from a fall out of a tree or one of several bike wrecks. A kid who is on a first name basis with the receptionist at the doctor's office, a kid known internally at that office as a "frequent flyer." A kid who, before their tenth birthday, has to use the back side of the form and a blank sheet of paper to complete their medical history. A kid who averages 2.5 bloody noses a week and has a designated puke pail under their bed. In our family, that kid was me.

It pretty much started at birth. I came into the world kicking and screaming with no doctor around to deliver me at 3:00 AM. My older brother, who weighed over 10 pounds at birth, had been a picture of health. I was the baby with colic, and I was inconsolable. My mom tells me that I pretty much cried all day and all night long. My folks tried every baby formula known to man in an effort to calm me down, but nothing worked. In an act of desperation, and defying conventional medical practices, my mom finally put me on whole milk, straight from the cow to my bottle. It worked! Still, growing up, I was a walking insurance claim.

I don't remember how old I was, but my many ailments led me to become somewhat obsessed with dying at an early age. I had convinced myself I would be one of those poor unfortunate souls to never reach adulthood. The only question was, "How would I die?" Would it be quicksand? I felt like lots of people in the movies and on television shows I was watching during that time were being sucked under by quicksand. If not quicksand, I was sure I would succumb to cancer. Movies like *Love Story* and *Brian's Song* haunted me, even though it was adults dying of cancer in those movies. My cancer self-diagnosis stemmed from how skinny and puny I was for my entire childhood and even into my early adult years. For the record, I did not weigh 100 pounds until after high school. I was scary thin, and I could tell family members and friends were very concerned about me.

"How skinny were you?" Thanks for asking. I was so skinny people in developing countries had pictures of me on their refrigerators. I was so skinny I kept getting Care Packages from UNICEF. I was so skinny UN helicopters would air drop food crates on my basketball court. I was so skinny I could hula hoop with a Cheerio. I was so skinny I could hide behind a fishing pole. And since all the pictures and movies of people I had seen dying of cancer were skinny, I was sure my time on earth would be short.

Eventually, my fear of dying from cancer diminished as someone suggested I might be living with a tapeworm in my intestine and explained how it could be coiled up as much as four feet long. To most people this would have been a horror, but for someone who was sure they were dying of cancer it became a beacon of hope. I named the tapeworm "Charlie" and enjoyed my new lease on life.

As I continued to lose weight, I was taken to a doctor who I distinctly remember saying to me, "I don't tell any of my patients this, but I want you to eat nothing but fat foods. I'm talking hamburgers, French fries, milkshakes, candy bars, ice cream, potato chips and all the stuff that makes other people fat." I always liked that doctor, and I wonder if he still has a practice. At the news of my new diet, tapeworm Charlie celebrated by doing backflips and, yes, the Worm Dance.

Turns out I did not have cancer or a tapeworm, but there were still many other ways I could die which had yet to be eliminated and needed my attention.

Influenced by Alfred Hitchcock's *The Birds,* I mused over the very real possibility the sparrows in my backyard would organize themselves and land on me and peck my eyes out, leaving me on the grass to die a slow death.

Recalling Bible stories and scenes from the movie, *Ben-Hur,* I entertained the thought of succumbing to leprosy. I didn't know anyone who had leprosy or ever died from it, but it didn't matter: I knew I would be the first in my family to contract it.

Somewhere along the line, I picked up another probable cause of death. Here's how it played out: a foreign and Communist government would invade our country and an evil soldier would put a gun to my head and ask, "Do you believe in God?" At which point I was supposed to say, with courage, "Yes I do." A single shot would be fired, and I would get my free ticket to heaven.

For a brief time, I was afraid of hippies, who I imagined belonged to an evil cult, would find their way to my hillbilly town, kidnap me, and then inject me with LSD. I would be found dead in an abandoned hippie van somewhere in California.

These and other myriad imagined maladies do not indicate a lack of real, unimagined ailments in my real life. My colic which had been cured by cow's milk was only the beginning of a series of health challenges. It started with chronic ear infections. I can still remember the excruciating and nonstop pain I endured for what seemed like my entire childhood. I can still feel my head resting on my mom's lap as she dripped ice cold drops from a medicine bottle into my ears. The cool liquid drops provided temporary relief, but I remember constantly scratching and digging at my ears in an effort to comfort myself. I recall the resultant bloody scabs and my mom's stern warnings: "You HAVE TO STOP digging at your ears or

it's going to get WORSE!" And then one night I believe I was the benefi-
ciary of a miracle. A man, who did not reveal is face, came to my bedside
and put his fingers in my ears and removed the scabs. And then he left.
When I woke up the next day I excitedly tried to describe to mom and
dad how a strange man had visited me in the night, removed my scabs
and healed my ear infection. While I am sure I had more ear infections
after the miraculous visitation, I can honestly say I don't remember my
ears being an issue after what happened that night.

At about this same time in my life, I was playing with some of my
mom's jewelry, which I had spread over her bed. While chewing on the
top portion of a hat pin, I somehow managed to swallow it whole. Mom
rushed me to the doctor's office where we were assured "everything
would come out in the end." Two days later I pooped out the hat pin, but
it would not have taken much for there to have been a much different
outcome.

At the age of eight I was playing "cops and robbers" with my brother
and some friends. Because my wrists were the size of candlesticks, they
secured both of my hands in one handcuff, attached the other to my belt
loop and ran away as fast as they could. The binding limited my movement to an awkward run, and in my effort to catch them, I fell to the
ground and broke my collarbone. Only it didn't feel like a collarbone: it
felt like I had broken my neck. I ran home screaming like a madman, "Oh
my God, I broke my neck!" (You've probably already concluded I can be
a little dramatic at times.) In my surgery, doctors placed a pin to join the
broken bones but less than two months later while wrestling around with
my brother I snapped the pin loose. The floating pin manifested itself as
a lump near the top of my shoulder and when I was taken to the family
doctor, instead of ordering an X-ray, he sent me home saying I had a post
operation cyst which would go away in time. I spent a painful summer
in a sling and on the day the doctor was to remove the "cyst" which had
not gone away, he decided to do an X-ray which revealed the pin, which
by now was almost pushing through my skin.

Some things just go together: chocolate and peanut butter, popcorn and movies, and, most relevantly to my childhood, bike wrecks and boys. For whatever reasons (maybe I was afraid I would die) I was a late bloomer in learning to ride a bike. Not being able to ride placed great limitations on adventures my brother and others my age could have during the summer months, so they simply went on without me. I was becoming a spectator to other people's fun.

Behind our house in a field where horses and cows ate grass was a huge and steep hill which was a blast to ride bikes down, or so it appeared. My brother and visiting boys would start at the top and, letting gravity do the work, pick up remarkable speed as they rode the bike to the foot of the hill. My brother even put ramps at the bottom of the hill which allowed cool stunts and serious "airtime."

I remember the fateful day my cousins were over to ride bikes down our hill. As I was watching them speed down the hill, enjoying a life I was sure to never experience, I got called out. "Hey, don't you know how to ride a bike yet?" This was the gravest insult a twelve-year-old boy can get, no matter how true its implication.

Before I could get out a shameful response, my brother rescued me. "He can ride with someone on the back!" This was not a true statement, but with the only ounce of pride I could muster I walked up the hill as if I were a decorated army general preparing to plant a victory flag on top of a conquered battle hill. My fear of being shamed had caused my pride to override common sense, and I nervously straddled the bike, not remembering how to steer, peddle, or even apply the brake while my simpleton cousin got on behind me.

I don't remember much of what happened next. With only training wheel bike experience, I, along with my "what was he thinking" cousin, made our fateful descent down the hill. Halfway down the hill my cousin shouted, "Let me off!" But it was too late.

As it turned out, we didn't need the brakes. At full speed the bike tipped over and my left elbow landed square on an exposed and embedded rock. Thus ended our ride and any notion I could, in fact, ride a bike with someone on the back.

My cousin somehow escaped unharmed, but a Niagara Falls blood stream was pouring down my arm. The wound extended the entire width of my elbow and was so deep when I bent my arm, even a little, I could see the blue-ish muscles and tendons popping out like a giant eyeball. I ran home and was quickly driven to our family doctor's office. Dr. J (not the basketball player, but read on and you will see how I may have been better off with the hoop star attending my wounds) sewed up my wound and sent me home.

For my bravery/stupidity, I was rewarded with a rare treat of a hamburger, French fries, and a Coke from a local fast food place, but I couldn't even eat or drink. My elbow was throbbing and my fever spiked, causing me to feel sick. I showed no improvement the next day, so my mom took me back to Dr. J.

It's hard to describe what happened next without making you want to drop this book and kneel before the porcelain throne and lose your last meal. Dr. J reopened the stitches only to be greeted by a gush of brown and black fluid pouring from my wound. Realizing he had not thoroughly sanitized the cut the first time, he carefully cleaned the wound before sewing me back up. As he brought me out to my anxious mom, he commended her for bringing me back so quickly and made an off handed remark how gangrene can invade a person's body in a matter of only hours.

I knew I had narrowly escaped having my good left arm amputated, and while I didn't get a hamburger and French fries do over, I was just happy to not have been fitted with a hook for an arm that day. I imagined a hook would have been a huge blow to my already awkward social life. Two years later, I finally learned how to ride a bike just as my other friends were now learning how to drive tractors and cars.

Admittedly, broken bones, bike wrecks, childhood ear infections and phantom tapeworms named Charlie hardly make for "near death" experiences. No, my first true flirtation with death came in eighth grade, when I almost died exploring a cave.

The Crooked River Basin is one of the most cavernous regions in the United States with 131 named caves along or close to its shores. As you might imagine, caves and young boys are a match made in heaven, and with so many caves so close to home we were active spelunkers. My older brother had been in so many caves, I fancied him as a certified cave guide and trusted him with my life even after he had convinced me I could ride a bike if someone was on the back.

Our favorite cave was on my uncle's land; it was called Wind Cave because of a breeze which seemed to blow in your face from the time you entered the cave until you came out. During the rainy months and times of flooding, the cave had a mini river flowing throughout it and a pool of water over 90 feet deep at the mouth of the cave which you had to carefully navigate around as you first entered. Some of my greatest adventures in life happened in Wind Cave. (I should probably also tell you Wind Cave was a great place to take girls.)

It was late fall and the leaves had long since fallen from the trees and formed a gray and crackly carpet beneath our feet as we entered the woods heading to Wind Cave. I made my way, along with my brother who had led dozens of friends through the cave, my uncle, and hippie whose name was Richard, down a steep slope when I realized that we had some-how gotten off track. Instead of coming into the mouth of the cave from a gentle slope and then up a creek bed, we were positioned way too close to the summit of the cave opening. And then it happened. I slipped on the leaves, landed on my butt and began sliding feet first down the side of the cliff. Like a kid going down a slide he never wanted to be on in the first place, there was no way I could stop, and rather than being greeted at the bottom by the arms of a loving parent, playground cedar chips or cushy green grass, I was plunging over the side of twenty foot cliff to be welcomed by giant moss covered boulders.

I have often heard people who share "near death" experiences talk about how they felt like they were floating in air just before the trauma, like a scene from a movie in slow motion. I honestly remember nothing about my landing except lying on top of a huge boulder and touching my head and seeing blood on my hand and then someone's plastic flashlight falling from the cliff and smacking me in the face even as I was trying to figure out if I were dead or alive. I felt like Wile E. Coyote in a Road Runner cartoon, whose reward for standing dazed but upright after a fall off a mountain was a giant rock right to the head.

Upon seeing my horrific fall, my brother did a Tarzan type swing from a tree and was at my side in a hurry. Hippie Richard's attempt to do my brother's Tarzan move ended up more like a George of the Jungle move and resulted in a broken hip. My uncle navigated a safer path down the side of the cliff to the creek bed where now half of our spelunking team was down for the count.

Together, we limped to the mouth of the cave, dipped our shirts in cold cave water and applied them to our wounds. Because we were Crooked River Boys we considered going through the cave in spite of our injuries, but the group decided Hippie Richard would have been too heavy to carry and I was struggling to remember what day it was.

As I look back on the events of that day, I still can't explain how I fell from such a great height and onto such big rocks with only a small scratch on my head (My, wife would like to add here: "and some brain damage"). My only explanation, and this is going to sound weird or overly spiritual to some, is that like a fireman catching someone from a burning house, God somehow caught me that day and cushioned my fall.

Having survived my cliff fall, I enjoyed a relatively healthy four years of high school. I was still scary skinny and had a tumble or two which required stitches (thankfully Dr. J had retired by then), and of course I contended with the common illnesses and parasites that most Crooked River people did.

Upon graduating from high school, I enrolled at a small institution called Ozark Christian College in Joplin Missouri. Little did I know before I was halfway through my first semester, I would encounter my next "near death" experience.

I was sitting in an 8:00 AM class slouching over my hard briefcase which sat on top of my desk waiting for the last few minutes of the class to tick off the clock when I straightened my torso only to experience a sharp pain in my chest. The pain literally took my breath away. I quickly bent back over and tried to straighten up again: same result. I actually thought I was having a heart attack at 18 years old (which makes sense because it had never before been on my list of how I would die).

Like the hunchback of Notre Dame, I made my way across campus doubled over and gasping for small whispers of breath. I rolled onto my bed in excruciating pain, hoping it was something which would pass, but it didn't. In desperation I went down to see our dorm mom, a four-foot-nothing woman whom we believed to be a contemporary to Moses. She must have relished for the first time having an eye to eye conversation with one of the men in the dorms she watched over. As I described my pain she responded with, "When was your last bowel movement?" Standing there, barely able to breath, I knew I needed a second opinion.

Eventually I ended up seeing the college nurse who listened to my chest and knew something was wrong. She sent me to the ER at St John's hospital (the one the tornado destroyed in 2011). After my chest X-Rays, the technician came into my room and announced I had experienced a spontaneous pneumothorax. "A numo what?" I said. And then he told me that, for no apparent reason, one of my lungs collapsed. This was shocking, to say the least, because for my whole life I had been an athlete and had only taken one puff of one cigarette (sorry mom); and, yes, I did inhale, which was why I have never taken another puff of a cigarette since.

The mystery of the causes for collapsed lung was as complicated as the procedure for the cure. I said to the ER guy, "So put a hose in my mouth or whatever you need to do to air up my lung and I'll just go back to enjoying my college career." He just looked at me and said, "We have to admit you into the hospital."

The next thing I knew, I was being wheeled up to the only room available, which was on the urology floor, because some days nothing goes right. Have you ever had one of those days where nothing went right? If you have, you know that things tend to get worse before they get better. Things got worse from there, way worse. I was fit into one of those hospital gowns without a back and was lying flat on my backside when the ill-tempered Dr. Stenson entered the room. Without as much as a "Hello" or "How are you doing?" Dr. Stenson gave me a local anesthesia injection in my upper chest and began making a small incision.

What happened next is not for the faint of heart. Without any explanation and before I knew what was happening, the six-foot three-inch 250-pound Dr. Stenson was leaning over the top of me, sticking a rod through the incision into my chest! He was putting his weight and downward pressure on it and moving it from side to side. I felt like a cowboy in one of those Western movies who had been shot with an arrow, but instead of trying to pull it out he was pushing it in further. I thought the rod/chest tube was going to come out of my back! When he finally got it into position he went to the foot of my bed and turned on a machine and walked out. I was pretty sure he didn't have any framed certificates on his office walls for bedside manners.

While in the hospital I was told it was possible my lung would inflate in a couple days and I would be released to head back to classes and college life. A couple days turned into ten days. After my first week at St John's Hospital it became clear I would not be able to return to college. I had not felt well enough to keep up with the heavy load of classwork. I was devastated.

In the midst of this emotional nadir, some of my high school friends made the nearly three-hour drive from Crocker to Joplin to visit me in the hospital. My joy rose as they all entered the room and started joking around with me about whether I was flirting with the nurses. As they lingered and laughed at my bedside, I began to start feeling weaker and weaker. My breathing became a little more labored and I saw what looked like blood backfilling into my chest tube. I looked down and sure enough, one of my hick friends was standing on the hose that led from my chest to the machine at the foot of my bed. Sometimes things go so badly you just have to laugh.

Speaking of laughing and nurses, I did in fact have a beautiful nurse who came to my bed bright and early every morning to sit me up and position me for my chest X-ray. The only problem which threatened any romantic move a guy with a collapsed lung could put on an attractive nurse can be described with two words: morning breath. I came up with a clever idea. My parents had left some hard candy at my bedside which meant all I had to do was wake up just before the beautiful nurse came in, suck on some fruity candy for a while and before you knew it we would be picking a wedding venue and china patterns and the names of our children. The morning came and I successfully woke up at dawn. I selected a grape sour ball and began frantically working it around the inside of my mouth in preparation for my love connection.

The next thing I remember the beautiful nurse was leaning over me saying, "Darin, can we get you ready for your chest X-ray this morning?" I was all out of sorts wondering what had happened and then I saw it. A purple puddle of sour grape drool on my pillow and on the front of my backless hospital gown. I had fallen asleep with the grape sour ball in my mouth. Now I was a purple drooling patient with morning breath. Our relationship never recovered.

Eventually I was released from the urology floor of St John's hospital and returned back home to Crocker where I hung out for a week or so before returning to college where I audited my classes for the rest of the semester. The thought of quitting college just because I had missed almost a month was not an option, even though I had to, eventually, retake all the courses I had started.

Recently, I was getting my haircut by Leanne, who grew up in Vietnam. I like Leanne because she remembers all the things we talk about from previous haircuts. Leanne likes to cut hair and Leanne likes to talk. The more Leanne talks the shorter my haircuts turn out. As Leanne was cutting my hair, she noticed the hairless bump on the right side of my skull and assured me it looked fine and wasn't that noticeable, which of course is a kind lie. And then I decided to tell her how I got the bump. I told her about my cave adventures as a kid. I explained how my brother took us down a wrong path and how I slipped and fell. I told her about hitting my head on the boulders.

As I was telling the story my audience was growing larger. The hair-stylist next to me was listening as was the lady in her chair. Other stylists who were waiting for clients were also engaged in my story. As Leanne unbuttoned and removed the body sized bib that catches hair, I got up out of the chair and while reaching for my wallet I announced, "I feel like God caught me that day. That he somehow cushioned my fall." And then I paused for effect while everyone was still listening and said, "I think God must have a plan for my life."

CHAPTER THREE:

DEAR ACCEPTANCE

Grind me, crush me, beat me.
But low I shall not lie.
I shall bounce back with much more fervor
and my zeal shall touch the sky...
-Neelam Saxena Chandra

While most people would rather have treble fishhooks pulled through their eyelids than go back and relive their adolescent years, I would like to give it a try, but only if I could take back the lessons I've learned with me. A popular saying which I think ended up in a country song expresses it this way: "What I wouldn't give to be younger and wiser."

When reflecting on their teen years, many people use expressions like, "I don't even know how I got through those years." Or, "Somehow I survived that period of my life." Or even, "I did so many foolish things back then, I'm lucky to be alive!" Many of our Crooked River stories can be traced back to the transitional time in our lives when we were desperately trying to figure out who we were and how to find the thing we wanted more than anything else in the world, acceptance.

In many ways, life was very good for me from 1976 to 1982. It was during this time I became a skilled angler able to cast my Zebco 33 with a beetle spin lure on the end of the line to within inches of the shore or near a log or submerged rock beneath the surface of the Crooked River. Few joys compare to the perfect cast of a fishing lure, the tension of a bite on the line, the quick set of the hook, and the reeling battle to land that keeper bass or even a large blue gill. For those who've never experienced it, I can only describe it as sheer, unadulterated, invigorating joy. My teen years were filled with day-long fish harvesting float trips on the Crooked River. Additionally, we had VIP access to dozens of farm ponds owned by my dad's boss, a guy named Winston, which is a very manly name. I think Winston appreciated my dad's hard work in the tire shop over the years and allowed him, and us, access to dozens of small and large ponds fully stocked with largemouth bass and some of Missouri's biggest blue gill. Very few people were allowed to fish in these ponds teeming with hungry fish just waiting to be caught. On a regular basis, my dad would take our family to Winston's Ponds where we would catch so many fish it was all I could do to keep our haul from dragging on the ground as we walked from the ponds across the grassy meadows back to the truck I can still feel the sting of the nylon stringer cutting into my palms as I struggled to carry our bounty almost a mile back to the truck. The pain never mattered, though, because I can also feel the satisfying heft of the fish hanging from the stringer and the pride that weight inspired. My dad called these great collections of fish "Pool Hall Stringers," which meant we would take them to the only watering hole in my hometown of Crocker and show off our fishing skills to the locals as they shot pool.

It was also during my adolescence I learned how to hunt cottontail rabbits. My dad was smart enough to know not to put a powerful shotgun in the hands of a ten-year-old, so I started my hunting career, as many young Crooked River boys did, with a BB gun. But my first kill was not a rabbit. My dad had convinced me that the multitude of innocent sparrows that dotted the many trees on our small farm carried a deadly disease which threatened our family's survival. Armed with my BB gun I daily took it upon myself to protect my family by terminating the lives of as many vicious, flesh-eating and disease-carrying sparrows as possible, but alas, the sparrows proved to be elusive and I, as the hick expression goes, "Couldn't hit the broad side of barn." Then it finally happened. A sparrow landed on a high branch of a tree in my backyard and I picked him off. The bird fell to the ground with a slight thud and I quickly snatched it up by its feet and carried my trophy into the house to show my mom. I can still hear her screaming, "Get that thing out here!" Having bagged my first game, I earned the trust of my dad and eventually graduated to a 410 shotgun and then on to a 20-gauge pump action shotgun. As I grew older, I realized I was only supposed to kill things for food, and while I did my share of providing rabbits and squirrel for my family to eat and enjoyed so many hunting trips, I was never as good a hunter as I was a fisherman.

Along with hunting and fishing, my involvement in team sports provided great and lasting memories. Our small-town school could not support a football team, but that didn't stop a small group of teenage boys from meeting together on most Sundays after church in the fall for tackle football. We didn't have any pads or helmets, and since I was, by far, the smallest guy on the field, I had a weekly goal of just not getting killed. When I caught a pass, I would often either run out of bounds or fall to the ground in the fetal position and yell, "I'm down!" My older brother, Troy, threw a pretty good deep ball back in the day, and I was on the receiving end of quite a few touchdown passes, which was another way I avoided being sent to the Emergency Room by guys who were twice my size. We also enjoyed our fair share of basketball, and, eventually, a very success- ful basketball coach was hired for our school's team. However, Coach Gray did not like his star basketball players risking injury while playing tackle football with no equipment. His ultimatum resulted in the end of my fun times playing pick-up football on crisp fall Sunday afternoons. For the record, we had great basketball teams during Coach Gray's time at our high school.

Summers in my small Crooked River town were all about Little League baseball. Beginning in elementary school and throughout middle school, I played on some championship teams which often finished the season with only a few, if any, losses. I batted leadoff, and because my small size resulted in a small strike zone, I took a lot of walks. When I wasn't walking, I would often lay down a near-perfect bunt and scamper to first base. After getting to first base, my speed usually allowed me to steal second and third. Then, it was only matter of time before the real hitters drove me home. I was a decent fielder with an above average throwing arm, but our pitchers were so good I rarely saw the ball come my way. I do remember being in perfect position in center field and catching a line drive against our rivals from Waynesville, who always posed the biggest challenge to our team. I also remember catching a soft pop fly ball while playing second base with two outs to secure a win for my team. Little League baseball on a dusty field under the Friday night lights was a memorable part of my Crooked River life, and playing the game scored me both team trophies and individual accolades, but the real joy was just playing with friends.

As fun as Sunday afternoon football and Friday night baseball were, my true love was basketball. When I was first learning to play, my dad nailed a faded orange and net-less rim about eight feet off the ground to our barn. At the time it was the best he could do, and I had to learn to dribble a ball on uneven ground and around rocks and cow patties. I desperately needed an upgrade if I was to become a basketball star. One of my most vivid memories of my teen years (and the greatest gift I have ever received) was the Saturday we mixed and poured concrete for our home basketball court. Before the end of the day, we had the twenty-by-ten concrete slab finished. We had also made use of a telephone pole upon which we attached a freshly painted plywood backboard and new, bright orange rim complete with a net. When the pole finally got stuck in the ground and cemented in place, I was the happiest person on the face of the earth. That small court would not only become a place I would spend countless hours of my life, but it also served as a safe place where I could go and be free of so many of the demons which were beginning to haunt me. The basketball court was not perfect. Too often the ball would hit the elevated corner of the court and bounce over the barbwire fence and into a gully which always seemed to be wet. I also had to shoot over a clothesline, which was even harder when my mom was drying clothes, and there was a small peach tree I had to shoot over in the back-left corner of the court. Still, I spent long hours perfecting my sweet left-handed jump shot on that court. Even darkness could not keep me off the court. We somehow landed a used lighting fixture which I powered by a long extension cord to my parent's bedroom and positioned in the peach tree perfectly aimed at the rim. My greatest moment on my home court came on the day my cousin, Kenny, who was a starter for our high school team and a very good player, came home from a week of basketball camp and I beat him in a game of one on one. I will carry that victory to my grave, even though he came back several times and I never beat him again.

My countless hours of practicing and pretending I was the latest NBA star on my home court never really translated on my middle school or high school teams. Although I was a great shooter, my size dictated that I play point guard, and because of turnovers I ended up on the end of the bench. I do remember swishing a game-winning 35-foot jumper in 9th grade, but more often than not, I simply watched others play the sport I loved from the bench or the bleachers during practices. Then, during my senior year, I did something Crooked River People hardly ever do. I quit. I took my folded-up uniform into the coaches' office and handed it in. It was like a scene from a movie and I remember being very emotional even as the coach lamented about not getting me into any games. As it turned out, quitting the team wasn't as hard as I thought it would be, especially when I considered there were rabbits to hunt right across the dirt road from my house, and I could still play basketball on my concrete slab anytime I wanted to.

As important and impactful as sports were during my teen years, there was another dimension of my life which dramatically changed me and shaped me into the person I am today. Although far from perfect, I grew up in a family who tried their best to follow Jesus. We fought, and we didn't always care for each other in loving ways, but we seemed to always forgive each other and quickly get back on track. Growing up, we attended Sunday School and church services on Sunday mornings. We went back on Sunday nights under kid protest because we had to miss the television program *The Wonderful World of Disney*. We frequently attended "Midweek Bible Study and Prayer Time" on Wednesday nights, and during the summer I attended a week-long program called "Christian Service Camp" at a location which was named after the Crooked River. It was here my life was forever altered. I was in middle school and had been thinking about becoming a follower of Jesus, which involved being baptized. For what seemed like a couple years I had watched other young people like myself, some even younger than I was, be baptized, but I was hesitant. I didn't want to stand up in front of people and be asked to say something while the whole church looked on.

It was a tradition in our church for people desiring baptism to come to the front of the church during this song called the "Invitation Hymn." The song, which changed every week, and the appeal to be baptized were given at the end of every Sunday service. I remember feeling the internal pressure to be baptized and to make public my decision to follow Christ. Every time the "Invitation Hymn" was played, I would grip the back of the pew in front of me, refuse to walk down the aisle, and convince myself I wasn't ready. Then one summer I attended the church camp, and one of the faculty members who was the most talented musician and coolest guys I had ever met asked me if he could share with me from the Bible how to become a follower of Jesus. I can still remember, with such clarity, sitting on this slanted wooden plank which served as a ramp to the boys' bunkhouse at Gasconade Christian Service Camp while David carefully, and with such ease and compassion talked with me about who Jesus was, what He had done for me, and how I could become His follower. The conversation with him that hot summer evening became a defining point in my life. When I returned home from camp, I told my parents I was now ready to accept Christ and be baptized. We went to the church office where we made plans for my baptism with our preacher whom everyone called "Brother Mac." The following Saturday, a traveling team from a local Christian college did a concert and at the end offered an "Invitation Hymn." There was no gripping the back of the pew this time. I went forward like I had been shot out of a cannon. I told everyone who had gathered at the church I wanted to give my life to Christ, and within minutes I donned a white linen robe, and my pastor, "Brother Mac" immersed me in the water, and I rose again to begin a new life. I can still remember the joy I felt that night and the warm hugs of people who greeted me after my baptism. It remains today the greatest decision I have ever made. And I made it as a teenager.

One would think with such a loving network of family, friends, church, and teammates, I would have never struggled with self-worth. But I did. Even though I was surrounded by a supportive family, a Christian community, and sports teams year-round my self-esteem began to nosedive in my teenage years. I can't pinpoint a specific time or event which caused me to begin to spiral down into a form of depression. It happened slowly and methodically. I think a big part of it was my appearance. I didn't like what I saw when I looked in the mirror. In terms of puberty, I was a late bloomer. I had no body hair and no muscles. I was so underweight people felt the need to comment on it from a place of feigned concern. My mousy brown hair laid flat on my head with no texture. My bottom row of teeth zigged and zagged like the fencepost on our property. I had a tooth pushed back on my upper row near the front which produced a huge gap which made me terribly self-conscious. It didn't help that one of the most beautiful and popular girls in my class would ask periodically, "When are you going to get braces?" The formula was simple math: bad hair + bad teeth + bad body = no girls interested in me.

Maybe I wouldn't have cared as much about the lack of a girlfriend if it weren't for the fact that, from my vantage point, it seemed everyone had one *except me!* Compounding the problem was my misfortune to have tasted the sweetness of love once and then been rejected. It happened, as many first kisses do, at a party when no adults were around. At an 8th grade basketball party, a guest room had been designated as "the kissing room," and after a few guys had emerged with big smiles on their faces it was my turn. I went into the dark room and before I knew it a cheerleader named Denise was sticking her tongue in my mouth and then, just like that, it was over. I remember thinking two things when I left the room. First, I remember thinking that what I had just experienced was something I definitely wanted to do again. My second thought was how the taste of Doritos was still awesome even coming from someone else's mouth. The next day I was sure Denise would ask me to be her boyfriend. Instead, she was only concerned about her performance. Apparently, what had been a first kiss and game changing moment for me had only been a warm up for her, and now she was moving up to the big leagues where she could score with high school guys who had great hair, straight teeth, and big muscles.

I did not respond well to the rejection I was experiencing from girls and my plummeting sense of identity and value. I turned inward and started to prefer being alone. I started isolating myself from others whenever I could. I spent hours listening to music – mostly sad love songs – on and old AM radio which picked up WLS in Chicago on a clear night. The music I was listening to made things worse. At my lowest point, Eric Carmen's song, "All by Myself" became my anthem. While my older brother listened to KISS and had a frightening poster of them on the wall near his bed, I listened to Barry Manilow, Bread, and the Bee Gees. I would obsess over certain single girls only to watch as they were swept off their feet by some guy who was better looking or more athletic than me. I was inconsolable. My parents tried to relate real stories of how they experienced the same things I was going through but I brushed them off. Adults at church offered platitudes like, "God has someone very special chosen just for you," which every single person knew was the kiss of death.

To compensate for my self-loathing and dark depression, I did things over a period of a few years I am not proud of. Things I wish I had never done. Things I wish I could go back and fix. Things for which I am deeply sorry and wish I could apologize for. Because I've always had a quick wit and sharp sense of humor, I turned my pain into hurting others by becoming a verbal arsonist. I made fun of others. I made up cruel names for people which unfortunately stuck to them. I criticized and laughed at people's physical flaws and championed others to join my cruelty. A classmate who peered over the top of his glasses reminded me of a puppet on the television show *Captain Kangaroo*. The puppet was named Mr. Rabbit, so I dubbed my classmate "Rabbit" and lead chants like Elmer Fudd in an episode of "Bugs Bunny" to "Kill the Rabbit." Or, more precise "Da Wabbit". A bucktoothed girl with bad fashion sense drew my attention and got tagged as "Cavewoman." Even my own sister, Kristan, was on the receiving end of insults and rude comments about her hair and weight during a critical time of her emotional development. I laughed and made others laugh, at the expense of my victims all day long at school, and then, alone on my bed at night, I would cry myself to sleep. I remember on one occasion being so depressed and feeling so bad about myself that I took the weights off of one of my dumbbells and began hitting myself repeatedly, trying to give myself a black eye in hopes someone would notice me and give me the love and acceptance I desperately needed. Another time, after being rejected by another girl, I started taking sedatives and even had thoughts of taking my own life.

It was during this time my young faith and efforts to follow Jesus were in shambles. I kept showing up to all the church and youth group events and pretending to be a good Christian, but away from those environments I was known more for my foul mouth and dirty and even racial jokes. As the poster child for hypocrisy, I began to hate my own duplicity, which caused even greater depression. I felt so lost.

Just like I can't remember a day or event which triggered the onset of my self-hate and depression, I don't recall a tipping point or significant event which brought me out of it. I strongly believe the culmination of my Crooked River upbringing and the cluster of relationships which surrounded me and never let me go or stopped loving me were the difference. But it took a while. Although I never heard God's audible voice, I had a sense He was continuing to challenge me to get off the fence and decide whether I wanted to follow Him. At some point in my senior year of high school I was finished being a faker and I was sick and tired of trying to get people to accept me. Over a period of a few months I experienced what I called a "second conversion." I ditched my plan to join the Navy, and when our church closed a Sunday service honoring me and my fellow High School Graduates with a song at the end of the service inviting people to the front of the stage to make a decision or ask for the church's prayers, I went forward and stood before the church and asked them to pray and support my decision to attend Bible College.

Even at Bible College my self-esteem and depression issues resurfaced after a few weeks into my Freshman Year but by this time I had learned how to study the Bible on my own and I had begun writing my prayers and struggles down in the form of prayers like King David did in the Bible book called Psalms. After attending and then graduating from Ozark Christian College, I began to see my true self restored through godly friendships; I developed my personal walk with God and got outside of myself through serving others. A few years after graduation from Ozark, the predictions of those who once offered that "God has someone special just for you" actually came true as I met a very beautiful, smart, and amazing woman who became my wife. Together, we shared the joy of bringing up two incredible daughters. As they grew up and began to experience what I had struggled with during my own adolescence, I tried to offer them something more creative than the stump speech, "I went through the same exact thing when I was your age" which parents often resort to. I wrote a song. The idea for the song came from a blog in which the author was writing an open letter to an invisible yet constant companion which he identified as the oppressive need to always be accepted by others. If you hear a little Taylor Swift influence in the mood of this work, it's because when I wrote it she was in the midst of writing smash hits which were based on her true life "break up" stories. Since my girls were fans, I decided to channel my inner Taylor Swift and write my own "break up" song.

Dear Acceptance

This letter is long overdue
I'm like the victim going back to their abuser
Hoping they'll change but they never do

What I'm trying to say is that "We're finished"
"I'm done with you"
And I don't want to "just be friends"
There's no reason to talk things through

Chorus

Dear Acceptance, I'm tired of playing all your games

Dear Acceptance, I'm stepping off your center stage
Dear Acceptance, you don't own me any more
Dear Acceptance, here's your coat, find the door

Everything you promised me ended up being all wrong
Posted pictures, changed my status, downloaded your favorite song

And I got so lost trying to find myself, a thousand miles off course
All your friends, pretending, all the partying only made it worse

I'm sick and exhausted of trying to be so interesting
I'm takin' off the pathetic sign asking everyone to "like me"

I tried the cool clothes and did whatever I needed to fit in
So what's with this cloud of shame? Why do you always win?

The approval of an invisible crowd no longer drives my life
I'll never be what you want me to be. Get lost. Good-bye

And I know you think that I'll be back, like a million times before
But I'm seeing someone else now and he's giving me so much more

The reality is our constant need for acceptance doesn't end with adolescence. It follows us into adulthood, and few things in life are more difficult to navigate than the feelings of being unwanted and unloved. Tragically, many people don't travel these waters very well, and some completely capsize and take others down with them. Persevering through self-esteem and depression is one of the most difficult things we do as humans. We need each other and we need Jesus who is the "someone else" at the end of my song. From my experience, he alone, can give you **so much more.**

CHAPTER FOUR:

MS. GASCONADE

It is said in some countries trees will grow, but will bear no fruit,
because there is no winter there."
-John Bunyan, *Seasonable Counsel, or Advice to Sufferers,* 1684

D onna was born and grew up in Upstate New York, nearly a thousand miles away from the crooked Gasconade River. But the river's
winding and persevering stream gladly welcomes her into the company
of overcomers who, despite what life throws at them, hold on to God
and refuse to quit or even consider abandoning their faith. This is her
Crooked River Story.

On **March 13, 1961**, Elnora and Paul welcomed Donna, their fifth of
seven children, into the world. Seven children were born into the Wind-
hausen family in eight years! According to family lore, Paul was eventually told that unless he wanted another mouth to feed, he shouldn't even
hang his pants on the couple's bed post. Providing for a family of nine
with a single income was no small task. Paul worked construction-type
jobs and eventually found steady income working for an asphalt paving
company, but the family barely got by. There was a time in Donna's childhood when all seven kids shared one bed, with four sleeping in one direction and three in the other. They had a working sink, but for a toilet they
used a ten-gallon plastic bucket with a toilet seat. Karen, the oldest, was
charged with carrying the waste to a big hole in the ground not far from
the family house. The family took baths in a big, metal washtub filled

with water Elnora heated on top of the stove. Quality meals were hard to come by. Donna remembers eating mayonnaise sandwiches for lunch and dinner more often than not and plain pasta with butter. She recalls a night when her dad brought home a hamburger and gave each child a bite and a couple of French fries. Many days, the children stood in line to receive a nasty tasting spoonful of cod liver oil to ensure they would not become malnourished.

The family traveled in a panel truck and the children sat on paint cans in the back. Occasionally on a Sunday after attending church services they would stop for Colossae cheese and chips at a store in Pulaski, New York. Donna and her sisters cut out and played with paper dolls from magazines and newspapers. The family occasionally received Christmas gifts from the Salvation Army. They wore each other's clothes to mix things up and Donna remembers wearing the same pair of yellow pants almost every day to high school. She never owned a pair of jeans until she moved away from home.

Donna graduated from Phoenix High School in three years and found a full-time job at a cable factory. She met and quickly fell in love with Dale. Donna and Dale were married at the Liverpool Christian Church near Syracuse, New York. They began married life in a humble apartment not far from her parents' apartment and the church building where they had been married. By early December, they had news they were expecting a child in March. As Christmas drew near Donna purchased a harmonica and a toolbox to give to Dale. These gifts represented the love she had for him and the future she hoped to share with him as her husband and the father of her unborn child.

On a cold December evening, one week before Christmas, Dale was putting on his snowsuit and boots in the hallway just inside the front door of the apartment, preparing for a ride on his snowmobile. Donna watched her new husband getting bundled up like a kid excitedly preparing to go out and build a snowman. Dale was so focused on the thrill of riding he forgot Donna was watching him and was about to open the door when Donna smiled and said, "Give me a kiss before you go out there." And then she added jokingly, "We might not see each other again." The two shared a short but sweet kiss and a longer hug. Dale headed for his snowmobile and Donna retreated to the bedroom to get ready for her late afternoon shift at Eagle Comtronics.

At about 7:00 PM in the factory where she was working, Donna looked across the room and saw an unusual sight. It was her dad, Paul, and the church pastor, Don, walking toward her workstation. In that very moment she knew something terrible had happened. She knew Dale had died. She ran to the bathroom with her sister, Joan, following behind. According to the police report, the throttle on Dale's snowmobile stuck and he was unable to gain control or get off it before entering a busy highway where he was struck head-on by a car. He was killed instantly.

Back at her workplace, Donna began shouting; she wanted to see Dale's body. It was all her dad could do to physically restrain her and calm her down while telling her the accident had been so gruesome that she would never be able to see him. Even before they took Donna back to her parents' house, the local news had reported Dale's death and shown video tape of his body lying on the side of the road at the accident scene. For a long time, Donna could not find the strength to go back to the apartment she shared with Dale but eventually she went back and tearfully opened the Christmas gifts she had wrapped for him, which included the harmonica and toolbox.

Because of the season-long freeze, burials can't take place during the cold winter months in Upstate New York. Graveside services have to be delayed until spring when the ground thaws enough for coffins to be put in the ground. While Dale's body was being preserved for burial, Donna purchased a cemetery plot and a tombstone, and tried to redirect her thoughts and emotions to becoming a mom, but she wasn't doing very well. She moved back in with her parents and tried to heed everyone's advice about caring for herself for the sake of her unborn child, but it proved extremely difficult. She gained a hundred pounds during her pregnancy, and as her due date in March drew near, she wasn't feeling particularly strong. Still, the hope of having a son to always remind her of Dale gave her the emotional strength to get out of bed and persevere through her tremendous loss. It was also during this time Donna got even closer to her mom, Elnora, through the great care she was giving her daughter in her time of grief and pain. Donna's siblings had always teased her about how she was "mommy's favorite." Elnora's love for Donna during this time carried her upstream on the Crooked River.

Two weeks after her due date, on **March 26, 1980,** Donna was taken to the hospital by Joan to deliver her son, whom she had decided to name Shane. Donna endured a long and intense labor. The nurses had to give her oxygen because she was not breathing well, and they were worried about the baby's heartrate. When it came time for delivery, Shane's head would emerge only to go back in again, which made necessary his removal with forceps. Upon delivery Shane's entire body was blue for lack of oxygen, and he was quickly whisked away from the birthing room by medical personnel. Donna never even got to see or hold him. She never got to experience the closeness a new mom has with her child upon delivery. In that moment, much like on the night when her dad and pastor came and she knew Dale had died before they even told her, Donna knew Shane would never come home with her. Baby Shane had not only suffered birth trauma but also, it was learned in the hours after his delivery, major organ failure, seizures, and hydrocephalus (water on the brain). Shane could not breathe on his own and was put on life support. He would spend much of his unfairly, tragically brief life hooked up to a variety of monitors and tubes.

There are no words which can describe those next few horrible and hellish hours and days for Donna. In the wake of Dale's loss, the very thing she had held out hope for —this daily reminder of their love, their son —was now being slowly taken from her. In the early days after Shane was born, the family prayed intensely, day and night, for a miracle, but with each day Shane's condition only grew worse. Within a few weeks, it was determined Shane was brain dead. Doctors and Shane's pediatrician began calling daily trying to talk to Donna, but during this time Elnora was taking all the calls because they kept insisting, even demanding, that Donna make the heart wrenching decision to pull the plug and end Shane's suffering.

Donna had already made the decision to send Shane on to heaven with Dale when, on **April 8, 1980,** after only thirteen days of life, the hospital called Donna and reported Shane's fight was now coming to an end and he would not endure another night. The hospital staff encouraged Donna to come down and hold him and say, "Goodbye." Elnora, along with Donna's brother Paul, drove her down to the hospital in Syracuse. By the time they arrived, Shane had been removed from the incubator and Donna was asked to sit in a rocking chair to hold him for the first and last time. Shane's body had a blueish tone as Donna held him close to her face and whispered that she loved him. Her last words to Shane were, "Go be with your daddy and I will see you soon." After a few short minutes, a nurse helped Donna take a clipping of Shane's hair to keep. Afterwards, Donna gave Shane back to nurse and cried all the way back to the car.

A few days later, a combined gravesite service was held for Dale and Shane. Shane's body was placed in a white mailbox-sized coffin and set next to Dale's coffin as the grieving family paid their final respects. Then, after the service, and when everyone had left, Shane's body was removed from his casket. Those in charge at the site then opened Dale's casket and placed Shane's body on top of Dale's body so he could rest in peace in his daddy's arms.

Donna had now, over the span of less than 100 days, lost and then buried both her husband and her son; not surprisingly she entered a dark, deep, and prolonged depression. She didn't listen to music for a year. She couldn't even bear to be in the presence of young children, including her own sister's daughter, Danielle, who was just a few months older than Shane would have been. It was simply too painful for her to be around a child, having lost her own. The only anchor in Donna's storm during this time was her continued faith in God. Donna reached out to God through her prayers, she found comfort reading her Bible, she attended church even though she felt overcome by emotions at times, and she continued to follow Jesus the best she could. Although she had lost everything, she never turned her back on God.

Tragedy would strike Donna's life again on **April 27ᵗʰ, 1989,** when, after a brave and painful fight against a rare form of bone cancer, sweet Elnora, the backbone of the family and Donna's greatest support during her pain, passed away at only 52 years of age, leaving Donna without a mom and a best friend.

If there were a Hall of Fame for Crooked River People, Donna would have an entire exhibit dedicated to her life entitled "Ms. Gasconade." She is tougher than any person I have ever met, and if you are wondering how I know all the details and datelines of her story so well, it is because on **November 20, 1990,** Ms. Gasconade met me in front of an altar at North Syracuse Christian Church in Upstate New York, where we joined hands, made promises, exchanged rings, and became husband and wife.

Getting to the altar on that memorable November evening was the result of perseverance and God's plan. It's the stuff of another Crooked River Story.

No one, except God, would have ever put Donna and me together. I had moved from my small town in Crocker, Missouri, to Upstate New York in a giant leap of faith to pursue an unpredictable church ministry in a place I had never been with a small group of people I had never met. At the same time, Donna was still grieving the loss of her mom. Though we were in the same state, we were worlds apart and neither of us was focusing on being in a relationship.

After working full time selling sporting goods and toys at a department store and serving two small rural churches in Phoenix and Parish, New York, I was hired away to become the full time Youth Pastor at a growing congregation called North Syracuse Christian Church. I have a faint memory of setting up extra chairs for Donna's mom Elnora's memorial service, but I have no memory of seeing or meeting her.

A few months later, after teaching a half dozen high schoolers a Sunday School lesson, I exited the small classroom to the left of the church stage. One of my students, Chad, was with me when I first noticed

Donna as she took her seat in a pew with her dad in a middle section of the church auditorium. Because Chad and his family had been in the church for years, I quickly and excitedly asked him (with a dramatic pause between each word) "Who is that?" Chad shrugged his shoulders and was no help. I felt like my opportunity to meet Donna was slipping away. I responded with a confidence I never even knew I possessed when it came to meeting girls by saying, "Let's go meet her." With Chad as my wingman, I introduced myself to Donna for the first time, and though the exchange was brief and a bit awkward, I can still proudly say I met my wife at church.

Donna and her dad continued to attend church services, but I didn't go out of my way to pursue anything beyond the expected perfunctory Sunday morning greetings required of all pastors. Though Donna tells me she was interested in me from the time we first met, I honestly thought she was out of my league. She was so beautiful, and I reasoned she had way better options than me.

A few months later, I decided to attend a singles' retreat at a camp where other lonely hearts from area churches gathered in desperate hope to find a connection with someone, even if for just a weekend. As I was unloading my suitcase and making my bunk in the men's dorm, I looked down the hill toward the basketball court and saw Donna getting out of the car. She looked beautiful, as always, but my excitement was quickly doused when I saw the "movie star handsome" guy she was with join her to remove her suitcase from the trunk of the car they had ridden in. I remember thinking, "Great, the most beautiful girl I'll see all weekend is already taken." And then, "People who are already coupled up should be banned from attending Christian singles retreats!"

Later, as all the men headed to the dorm after the lights went out, I overheard one of the other guys talking to Mr. Movie Star Handsome Guy about his girlfriend. "How long have you two been dating?" asked the first guy. "Oh, no," replied Mr. Movie Star, "She is my sister". We all laughed, and I headed off to a hopeful night of sleep. Donna was in play!

Knowing Donna was not taken allowed me to loosen up a bit for the remainder of the retreat. We flirted a bit, and I could sense we enjoyed hanging out together. Still, my uncelebrated history of relationships with women gave me zero clues about whether she liked me and even less confidence to pursue anything once the retreat had ended.

At the end of the summer, after all the youth camps had ended, there was a final weekend camping event at the same site where the singles retreat had taken place. The event was called Family Camp, and area church members stayed in tents, RVs, cabins, and the bunk houses while sharing meals together at the cafeteria. There were Bible teachings and singing opportunities in the morning and evening along with free time for sports or rest in the afternoon. Each night ended with a bonfire. In the weeks leading up to Family Camp I was determined not to attend. I had decided that staying home and wallowing in depression while mourning how much I missed my family back in Missouri was the move. Besides, I was a single guy. The camp only had one weekend for my type of people, and it had already taken place. At the last minute, and because I lacked any semblance of a social life, I reluctantly agreed to jump in a car with a lady from church, Joyce, and Chad. Together, we headed to Family Camp. It turned out to be one of the best decisions of my life.

We parked the car on the verdant slopes of the camp parking lot, and as I grabbed my stuff to head up to the door to the men's dorm, I saw Donna gently swaying on a porch swing in the late summer breeze. This time, she was with her sisters Joan and Karen as well as her brother Paul (AKA Mr. Movie Star Handsome Guy). For reasons I could not explain but will forever be thankful for, Donna and her siblings adopted me as their newest family member, and everything lined up perfectly all weekend long for me to get to know Donna better. We sat together in the Bible teaching sessions where I noted how she opened her well-worn Bible filled with papers and notes she had taken over the years. As a pastor I found her interest in and devotion to God's Word attractive. As the weekend unfolded, we played volleyball, sat on the porch swing, looked up at the stars, and sat around campfires. We even took a turn doing the dishes, like all the other families, and our hands touched for the first time in a playful exchange of transferring dishes from a wash to rinse sink.

On the final night of Family Camp, I found a rose and placed it on the doorstep of the cabin where she and her sisters had been staying. It would be clear who had left it and who it was for. The next day I hugged Donna as we said goodbye. It had been the most incredible weekend of my life. And to think I almost didn't go.

I felt sorry for Joyce and Chad on our two-hour car ride back home. I was in love and I could not shut up about Donna. I even began singing, without stopping, the words to a song for which I only knew two words. The name of the song was "O Donna." I'm sure they were relieved to drop me back off at North Syracuse Christian Church. I continued to sing for my new love even as I crossed the church's gravel parking lot to my car to head home.

When I got back to my apartment, I knew I had to ask Donna to out on a date. The problem was I suffered from an under-researched phobia which I called "The fear of calling girls on the phone." I had been conditioned to this phobia over the course of many years. As a teenager, I had determined so many times to call any number of girls and just put myself out there and share my love for them or ask them to go out with me. I can remember so many times holding the yellow phone receiver in my hand, trying to find the courage to call my latest crush and express my undying love. But it never happened. Not even once. I always chickened out. Now, as a 26-year-old man, I was facing the same phobia. This time, though, my love for Donna allowed me to face the monster of my fear and make what would be the most important phone call in my life. My heart pounded as I pressed each number on the phone pad. After only a couple of rings, Donna answered. I remember saying, "Hi this is Darin," but before I could say another word she responded with, "Oh hi, can I put you on hold for just a second?" I politely answered, "Sure, no problem" and then I heard a faint click.

The phone technology at the time I had called Donna had advanced to an upgraded feature called "Call Waiting." Donna, who was living with her dad and sister Laura at the time, had just purchased the feature for their phone only days before my courageous call. As I waited for Donna to return to me, the seconds turned into minutes. After about five minutes I began to worry she had purposely hung up on me and was now in her room with a bunch of friends laughing at me even as she asked them how she could get rid of me. After ten minutes I began to lose hope but thought maybe it was some kind of cruel act to test my love and affection. After fifteen minutes I decided to hang up the phone, pack my bags, move back to Missouri, get a job preaching at a country church, plant a garden, and hopefully marry a local girl who had a full mouth of teeth.

Before I could start packing my bags, Donna called me back. She quickly apologized for having misused the "Call Waiting" feature and explained how they had just gotten the service and were not sure how to use it yet. I was just relieved she had not only called me back but also had to contact her brother Paul to get my number. This was an act of true love, or at least interest. We made plans for our first date. Two Crooked River People were beginning to travel the same stream.

I was nervous and excited as I drove the 24 miles from my apartment in Phoenix down to the south side of Syracuse and Donna's house on Durston Avenue. Donna navigated us through backroads to a diner in Mattydale called Zebb's for our first date. In the fall we joined her brother Paul and Karen for a day trip to the Adirondack Mountains to look at the beautifully colored trees. We drove to the top of Whiteface Mountain where I saw rows of yellow, orange, and red tree colors. It was as if God had carefully lined up each section using one of those paint by number sets. I had never seen such beauty. In the back seat on the way home, Donna and I held hands and shared soft and secret kisses. It had been one of the best days of my life.

The true measure of my love for Donna came a few months later as winter began its fierce assault on Central New York. When I first moved to New York, the residents there were surprised to learn I had a rear-wheeled drive car. They implored me to buy the best snow tires available and to put as much weight in the trunk of my car as possible for traction. They probably didn't consider their words as dating advice, but as I made the almost nightly drive down to Donna's house, their words certainly made the difference. During our dating period, Syracuse was recognized as the snowiest metropolitan area in the United States. I would drive down to Donna's house after work and stay way longer than a man of God should and then brush several inches of snow off my car before heading up to Interstate 81 and then Interstate 481. The snow squalls created whiteouts which made it nearly impossible for me to see if I was on the road. There were a few nights when it felt like I was the snowplow because I couldn't even see the evidence of tire tracks on the snow-covered road.

As Donna and I continued dating we opened up to each other about our pasts and our pains. Donna's tragic series of losses only served to make me love and want to be with her more, and as I shared with her my feelings of inadequacy and low self-esteem, she responded with under-standing, support, and affection. It became clear to us that we needed each other, and God had brought us together.

Exactly one year after our first date, a guy from our church who owned a limousine service drove us back to Zebb's and later to my apart-ment where I asked Donna to marry me. At that time, I couldn't afford a wedding ring (which I felt terrible about) but we decided to pull our resources together and plan our wedding which took place at North Syracuse Christian Church just a few months later.

There was never a more beautiful bride than Donna, but her beauty was more than just her dress and physical appearance. Allow me to borrow the words of Elisabeth Kubler-Ross: *"The most beautiful people we have known are those who have known defeat, known suffering, known struggle and have found their way out of the depths. These persons have an appreciation, a sensitivity and an understanding of life that fills them with compassion, gentleness and a deep loving concern. Beautiful people do not just happen."*

CHAPTER FIVE:

WHAT I LEARNED ABOUT LIFE AT A CAMP WHERE KIDS FOUGHT FOR THEIRS

We do not receive wisdom, we must discover it for ourselves, after a journey through the wilderness which no one can make for us, which no one can spare us.
-Marcel Proust, **Á la recherche du temps perdu,** 1913

During a particularly dry and depressing season of my soul, I asked God what He was doing outside my safe suburban bubble and the small church where I served as a pastor, and if, perhaps, he might direct me and let me join him.

Instead of having me pack my bags to serve the poor in some Third World country or tote my Bible and machete to some dense jungle to preach and convert lost souls, God led me to fill out an application to become a counselor at a camp for kids who were battling cancer. The organization was rightfully named Camp Fantastic, and the week-long experience was to be held at a beautiful 4H Camp in Front Royal, Virginia.

All my years of loving and serving young people in church camps and my background in sports got me through the application stage and to the in-person interview with the head guy at Camp Fantastic. I remember not playing the "I'm on a mission from God" card in my interview but rather simply promising to work hard and love the kids as best as I could.

Because of the unique health challenges of our campers, the faculty of Camp Fantastic arrived a couple days ahead of the campers for long days of training and getting to know each other. I could not have been more impressed with the group of mostly young adults who were all committed to care for these kids and give them the time of their lives. We were told the goal of the week was to try to help the campers take their minds off their medications and treatments and to get them away from hospital beds and doctor appointments and into some of the fresh air and fun times all kids should experience in the summer. Though still not fully knowing what to expect, I was excited and happy the day the kids finally arrived.

The kids, ranging in ages from 8-18, made the journey from the National Institute of Health (NIH) in Bethesda Maryland to the 4H Camp in Virginia on luxury tour buses and, much to my surprise and delight, accompanied by an escort of Harley driving, leather jacket clad motorcyclists. It was like nothing I had ever seen before. A true heroes' welcome. Dressed in a funny party hat, I joined other members of the faculty lined on both sides of the narrow asphalt road at the camp and applauded our new arrivals.

With little to no regard for their disabilities, the kids quickly exited one bus and rushed over to greet the kids from the other. Warm embraces were shared and kids smiled and laughed as they reunited with friends from previous years at Camp Fantastic. I had witnessed a similar scene before as kids from different churches ran across parking lots at church camps in my own youth group to see friends they had not seen from other youth groups for a year. What was different about this was there were some kids who were looking for old friends who had tragically passed away during the year. In our training, we were taught this could be a very emotional time for the kids. They might be thrilled in one moment to see a friend from last year and then suddenly grief stricken to not see someone they thought would return. To honor the memory of friends who lost their battle to cancer, Camp Fantastic allowed the children to plant a small tree overlooking a pond in memory of their lost friends. Though sad, it remains one of my greatest memories of the week. As I watched each kid get off the bus that day, I knew I was in the company of brave kids some of whom were clinging to life. Their lives, like the Crooked River, were about fighting and refusing to give up.

As its name suggests, the camp facilities and program were truly "Fantastic." I remember during my days of working at church camps in Upstate New York, I had a great friend and seasoned camp counselor, Mike, who always reminded me, "Camp is for the campers." It was his way of making sure all the faculty got on the same page of making every moment count and doing everything possible to provide a great and memorable experience for the kids. Camp Fantastic was "camp is for the campers" on steroids! Everything from the food to the accommodations, to the daily schedule, to the activities, the appearances by local celebrities, to the personal care was specifically designed to show these kids the time of their lives. As you might imagine, the faculty alone could not have cared for the kids and allowed for the experience without the help of a pretty substantial medical nursing crew. The group of nurses from NIH who supported Camp Fantastic was full of smiles and fun antics. I could truly tell they wanted to be there, and they loved these special kids dearly.

A typical day at Camp Fantastic included a variety of morning activities like archery, horseback riding, crafts, four square, basketball, martial arts and other options chosen by the kids. There were a couple of offsite field trips, evening activities and a roaring campfire to close each day. In between the activities were wonderful, "all you could eat" meals (including ice cream) and what we called "Med-line" where the kids receiving cancer treatments would go for their medications or injections from the nurses. The days were filled with so much fun that no one had to be told to turn out the lights and go the sleep at night.

Built into the daily schedule was some free time which would have normally been a great time to take a nap, but the two young boys under my 24/7 care wanted to swim *every single day.* It rained at least two days we were there during designated swim time. The rain on those two days was not the quick passing, thunder-and-lightning kind of rain, but rather the slow and steady rain which normally forces everyone indoors. On the first of these rainy days, I told my guys, "Well it's too bad we can't go swimming today." Five minutes later, they had their swimming trunks and flip flops on. And before you could blink, I had mine on as well. As we headed out the door of our cabin into the slow drizzle, I grumbled to myself something about how "camp is for the campers."

I was quite sure we would be the only ones at the pool on a rainy day. I mean, who goes swimming in the rain? But as we got closer, I could hear the sounds of children swimming. My boys starting walking faster, and as we arrived, I realized that, while no one from the local community was at the pool, almost the entire cancer camp population was!

The swimming pool we frequented every afternoon (even when it rained) was shared between the cancer camp kids and faculty and the general public. Actually "shared" is a bit of a misnomer, because once the wave of cancer kids came into the pool, most of the general public headed for the exits. If you had seen the scene, you would probably would have done the same.

The kids from the cancer camp were always extremely excited to get into the pool, just like all kids are, but before they could take their first plunge, they had to go through a medical screening process enforced by the NIH nurses. People receiving chemotherapy or radiation treatments for cancer are very vulnerable to sun exposure. Too much sun can be really harmful, even dangerous for them because they burn much quicker than others. Because of this, the NIH nurses formed an impenetrable barricade between the bath house exit and the swimming pool. Every kid from the cancer camp processed through this line where they received the total body coverage of sunscreen (SPF50). And by total body coverage I mean to say that, unless you looked like Casper the Friendly Ghost, you were not swimming. One could always locate the cancer camp kids in the pool because they looked like they had been covered in mayonnaise.

Adding to their ghostly appearance, some kids had plastic tubes from which they received chemo, taped to their chests. Other kids wore eye patches. Many of the kids, including girls, were bald or only had thin strands of hair. In their excitement to finally get through the NIH nurses border patrol and jump into the water some of the campers would forget all decorum and simply detach their prosthetic limbs and leave them against the chain link fence surrounding the pool in full view of everyone. When the cancer camp kids and faculty entered the pool area, we looked like a group of people who had just escaped from a hospital ward or Captain Hook's pirate ship. No wonder moms grabbed their children and ran for their cars when we came in.

It was at the pool where I witnessed perhaps the greatest example of perseverance I have ever encountered. I had jumped into chest-deep water when I was startled by a sudden splash just a couple of feet away. I saw beneath the surface of the water one of the kids from the camp. When she surfaced from the water the first thing I noticed was that she was one of the youngest of the cancer camp kids. The second thing I noticed was both of her arms had been amputated at the shoulders. My first thought was to go into my "David Hasselhoff-Bay Watch-Life Guard Saving Mode" because surely a young girl with no arms jumping into a pool of water over her head would quickly sink to the bottom of the pool like a rock. Turns out, she could swim better and longer than I could. She probably could have given Michael Phelps a run for his money! Her swimming style was a bit unorthodox. She didn't swim horizontally across the water, but rather her body stayed vertical as she twisted her upper body side to side like the inside of a washing machine and paddled her feet like she was riding a bike. Over the next couple of hours, I watched this young girl swim not merely a few laps across the pool, but around the perimeter of this giant community pool! Around and around she swam like the Energizer Bunny. No one was in the pool longer than she was that day and no one had to work harder just to keep her head above the water.

Later, when I was thinking about the incredible strength of this young girl, I had a flashback to the time I nearly drowned back when I was a teenager. My friends and I were wade fishing in the middle of the Crooked River, and I was holding my fishing pole in one hand and a minnow bucket in the other when I stepped into a hole in the riverbed deeper than I was tall; I was completely submerged.. Because of poverty and standard teenage bone headedness, letting go of either the fishing pole or the minnow bucket was not an option. I began paddling my legs as fast as I could to keep my head above the water. My minnow bucket was quickly filling up with water and serving as an anchor dragging me deeper into the water, but with great effort I was able to move about 10 feet and get out of trouble. Safely on the shore I bent over, trying to catch my breath, and wondered if I was going to pass out from exhaustion. Every muscle in my body was pulsating, my lungs were burning, and my hands felt numb still firmly gripping my fishing pole and minnow bucket. As I reflect on this today, the story reads like a Jeff Foxworthy joke: "If you've ever almost drowned trying to save a $10 fishing pole and a minnow bucket...You might be a redneck." It is also a testament to the young girl's strength I witnessed at the swimming pool. The experience of almost drowning from not being able to use my arms while swimming highlight not only the incredible physical strength of the young Crooked River Girl, but also the triumphant bravery she must have needed to learn to swim in the first place. Her courage, strength, and perseverance continue to inspire me to greater things today.

There was another camper who came to the pool every day, but she never swam. She looked to me to be the sickest person at the camp; I did not believe she had many days left. Her eyes were sunken into her head. Her face had a pale and grayish tint. Her body was thin and frail, and she always dressed as if she was cold. She wore a floppy hat to cover her bald head, and while she could stand and walk a bit on her own, she was too weak and spent the majority of her time in a wheelchair as a spectator to other people's fun. My heart just broke for this lovely girl in a battle for her life, and even though the camp had assigned two boys for me to entertain all week, I knew God had assigned her to my care as well... or was it the other way around?

All week long I tried to make a friendly and compassionate connection with this girl. I attempted to start up conversations with her and did anything I could to make her laugh. She was not amused, and I felt if I continued, I might become the first ever cancer camp volunteer to be served with a restraining order. She seemed annoyed by my very presence. Undeterred, I kept smiling and waving at her across the room. I went out of my way to open doors for her and do anything I could to help her. I got nothing in return until the very last night of the camp.

If you ask the kids at the cancer camp to tell you what they most look forward to during their stay at Camp Fantastic they would, without hesitation, tell you it is the Friday night dance. Every year, the faculty fire up a grand finale to the week of cancer camp by throwing a prom-quality celebration complete with decorations, amazing food, a DJ from DC, disco lights, photography; it was the real deal. The kids plan ahead and pack formal and semi-formal dresses and suits and spend the entire Friday afternoon (after swimming, of course) getting ready for their big night.

I remember feeling underdressed compared to the campers on the final night as I entered the lodge where the dance was taking place. I heard a slow song playing and then it hit me: I had one last chance to connect with the girl who had successfully avoided me all week long. I would ask her to dance. As my eyes scanned the room of other couples embracing and swaying to the music, I thought for sure I would see her alone in the wheelchair again watching others having fun like she had been doing all week. I almost gave up my search and then I saw her. There she was... *in the arms of another man!* He was much younger than I, and a fellow faculty member. He was tall, dark and handsome and had played college basketball at Drexel (I'm not sure why I remember that). With her back to me and in the embrace of this guy, who, like me was just trying to show this girl unconditional love, I courageously tapped her on the shoulder and as she turned around and looked at me I said, "I'm next!"

What happened next could not have surprised me more. She literally pushed her dance partner away and before I knew what was happening wrapped her arms around me and began to dance with me. I'm not a very good dancer. In fact, I subscribe to my dad's philosophy of dancing: "I can't dance, but I can hold on to those who do." And so that's what I did. I just held on. We didn't say much to each other. I remember asking her if she had enjoyed her week at camp but that was about the extent of the conversation. It wasn't about words. The dance with the bald girl at cancer camp at a 4H Lodge in Front Royal Virginia remains today as one of the greatest expressions of love I have ever received from another human being which was ironic because I thought I was going there to help them feel better.

Looking back on my experience at Camp Fantastic, I can see what God was teaching me. By observing these courageous kids, I learned to make every day count. To swim and have fun, even in the rain. I learned that if an eight-year-old armless girl could swim in circles around me all afternoon, I could find the strength and stamina to press through whatever obstacles I had to face. And finally, I learned from dancing with the bald girl how, sometimes, God plays tricks on us. We go to places or things to show love and serve others and instead find ourselves being the recipients of loving experiences we never saw coming our way and will never forget.

CHAPTER SIX:
PASTOR CHINO WORLDWIDE

Through hard work, perseverance and a faith in God, you can live your dreams.
-Ben Carson

One of the reasons I believe in God and in his direct involvement in my Crooked River life is because it is the only plausible explanation for how a dirt poor, small town kid like me could have spent thirty weeks of his life traveling to almost twenty different countries in all but two continents on the planet. People growing up near the Crooked River usually did not venture far from home. I can remember sitting on the railroad tracks as a young boy and wondering where the Frisco trains went. I even imagined myself jumping on a boxcar, like I had seen people do in the movies, and riding it for a couple of days just to see where I ended up. Back then, a couple days' train ride was the outer limits of my imagination in terms of the size of the world and my ever getting to see it.

The path from my Crooked River life to some of the largest, poorest, and most beautiful places in the world began in a very unsuspecting place. The Crocker Christian Church which my family attended from my infancy had a passion and a reputation for caring about and loving people all over the world. Every year the church hosted a month-long rally where missionaries and even natural born citizens from countries around world came to our church to either raise financial support for their work or to update the church on their activities. The global church workers usually brought these cool slide projectors with hundreds of pictures of people and scenes from all over the world. During the rally the church combined all Sunday school classes into the church auditorium and after a brief introduction, the missionaries called for the house lights to be turned off and transported us to countries far different from our own. In addition, the missionaries would often set up display tables in the church foyer with artwork, everyday items, clothing, and all kinds of handmade crafts from their countries. The event, which was called a "Faith Promise Rally," featured different speakers and different countries every week, and at the end of the month the church was always eager to make financial pledges to the missionary of their choice and to enjoy an all church celebration potluck dinner afterwards. The culmination of the rally came when a giant globe was placed off to the side of the stage encircled by a wooden sign with different dollar amounts representing the total amount our church would be giving to world missions that year. Each dollar amount had a red light bulb beneath it and a simple flip switch.

At the close of the rally, church members were given donor cards which were to be filled out and then handed in to be calculated. Two elders of our church, both named Junior, added up the pledge amounts and flipped the switches igniting the red light bulbs encircling the globe. I can remember watching this unfold as a kid and getting more and more excited with the illumination of each red bulb. The last dollar amount represented the yearly goal, which got bigger every year. Even as a kid who pledged only one dollar a month, I still felt like I was part of something big which was changing the world. Even into my twenties, after I had moved away, the church continued to hit their ever-increasing mission giving goals. It was one of the few churches in America where more dollars went out of the church than stayed in it. It's funny how such a small church in such a small, impoverished town gave me such a huge vision for the needs of others all over the world.

My path to worldwide mission work and travels continued as I enrolled in a small Bible college in Joplin Missouri called Ozark Christian College. It would have been impossible for me to have attended even a semester at this Christian worker training school and missed its global emphasis and impact. I was exposed early and often to missionaries during my time at Ozark. They preached in chapel, taught classes, and showed up in our dorms on a regular basis to inspire and challenge the next generation of global workers. At Ozark, we watched films about global missions, sang songs about the need for more workers, and dedicated an entire week on campus to mission emphasis.

One of the songs we sang during Mission Emphasis Week and during many chapel services was the song, "I'll Go Where You Want Me to Go". Though I couldn't imagine how or where God would send a small-town Crooked River Boy like me, I still sang my "tone deaf" heart out and felt every word of the lyrics:

"It may not be on the mountain height or over the stormy sea. It may not be at the battle's front My Lord will have need of me.

"But if, by a still small voice he calls to paths I do not know, I'll answer, dear Lord, with my hand in thine I'll go where you want me to do.

"I'll go where you want me to go dear Lord, over mountain or plain or sea. I'll say what you want me to say dear Lord. I'll be what you want me to be."

For many college students, spring break means booze and beach parties; for Ozark students, it means joining professors and peers on mission trips to share God's love in other countries and in underserved urban communities in the US. Ozark boasts that the sun never sets on one of their alumni; both current students and graduates represent Ozark in every corner of the map. At Ozark, I not only decided to become a pastor but also determined to help whatever church I ended up serving to have an active global presence, to serve the financial, physical, spiritual, and prayer needs of people from every tribe, tongue, and nation.

I cannot overstate how important my home church and Ozark Christian College were to my future adventures in global mission work. After graduating from Ozark, I eventually landed a position as a youth pastor in Syracuse, New York. It was during this time that Mike Bowers, a good friend and key player in my global story, suggested we should join an organization called Christ in Youth for one of their Youth Pastors Introduction to Short Term Mission Trips. During this time, it was very popular for youth pastors to take members of their youth groups on short (7-10 days) mission trip experiences often in Third World or developing countries. Mike was such a fun guy to be with, and since it was his first trip as well, I was all in for what would be the first of many foreign trips. The decision was made easier by the fact the trip was to the Dominican Republic in January. Those who know anything about winter in Syracuse will understand the Dominican Republic's Caribbean appeal.

I could not have picked a better place to begin my world travels and mission work. I quickly fell in love with the beautiful and joy-filled people of the Dominican Republic. On the trip (and the almost 30 subsequent trips I have been on since then), I saw how my Crooked River upbringing served me well in a variety of cross-cultural settings and challenges. It seemed like every experience had a number of twists and turns and sometimes scary moments just like the Gasconade River of my youth.

Travel to, from, and within these countries was almost always marked by sudden changes, delays, dangerous roads, and unmet schedules. After a few years of experiencing so many travel related issues I began to prepare teams for trips by telling them, "We're going to use the 'F' word a lot on this trip." Then I would pause for effect and say, "Flexibility." Traveling all over the world has left me stranded in airports, spending extra days in hotels where I didn't want to be, and hopelessly waiting along the side of many dirt roads waiting for a flat tire to get fixed or some other type of mechanical failure to be resolved. At a certain point, I didn't even count it as a real mission trip unless a vehicle we were traveling betrayed us with a flat tire or some type of engine issue. I have officially been stranded on the road on almost every continent, and on one trip set the modern missionary record of push starting a Jeep in three different countries on the same day. We had so many flat tires on the school buses our medical teams traveled on in Nicaragua we started adding the cost of tires to our "in country expenses" budget for the trip. In Managua after a morning of doing concrete work and while waiting for lunch to be served some of my new friends, through a translator, asked if I was Asian (for the record, due to my eye shape I get this in almost every country I visit and even here in the States). I laughed and told them I didn't think I was, but they insisted, and thus the lore of Pastor Chino began.

Other travel challenges included an impromptu game of soccer with some kids from a village on our way to Abidjan in the Ivory Coast while we waited 3 hours for a backup Land Rover to replace the one we were traveling in due to a clutch failure. I'm pretty sure we were their first white skinned guests they had ever seen in their neighborhood, but we had blast while making the most of a bad situation which was a feature of perseverance I had trained my teams to be prepared for on mission trips. In fact, it was often these unscheduled and serendipitous moments which we looked back upon as being the most significant experiences we shared on the trips.

Back in the Dominican Republic, I was in the back of the missionary's truck with what felt like 50 young people (probably an exaggeration but people from other countries sure know how to pack in a vehicle, and personal space is not really a thing) singing praises to God when a driving tropical rainstorm hit us. The good news: the truck had a camper shell. The bad news: the camper shell had so many holes the water channeled to the vehicle's roof above where I was sitting. Rainwater poured on me like it was coming out of a faucet. In the end I would have probably stayed drier in the open air with no camper shell. Eventually, it stopped raining and then, of course, we got the flat tire.

It wasn't just the travel issues which required my Crooked River perseverance. We always seemed to have more than our fair share of lost suitcases and baggage mix-ups; this was especially true when governmental corruption factored into the equation. The first couple of years, when we brought medical teams and their supplies into the airport in Managua, Nicaragua, we were greeted warmly and waved quickly through customs lines like returning family members of the guards. In subsequent years, the guards at the airport started combing through our stuff. Then one year, for reasons I could not explain, they simply seized all our medical gear and took it away. The next thing I knew, I was transported to a high level government building where, with the help of some guys from the local church, we negotiated a deal whereby the release of our supplies was contingent upon our agreement to host an unscheduled medical clinic for which the government, not the churches, would receive honor and gratitude from the community. We needed the supplies, so we made the deal.

Another memorable baggage issue came up on our return flight from the Ivory Coast to the US. One of our fiery female members had her name called over the load speaker just minutes before we were to board the plane. As she exited the boarding area, I could see her face getting red with anger. For a moment, I was paralyzed by the thought she would be detained and, as the leader of the team, I would need to stay back with her while the rest of the group boarded the flight home. Frantically, I stepped out of the boarding gate area and I was able to get her attention just before the guards escorted her out of the secure area. I said to her, "Remember to be nice!" Thankfully, after a few minutes and just before we boarded, she returned laughing about how they only wanted to ask her why she was returning to the United States with five machetes in her checked bag. She politely told the guards they were gifts. I was just glad she didn't try to use one on them.

After travel challenges in foreign countries come health concerns. It was always a little unnerving to read pages upon pages of health and disease warnings on the Center for Disease and Control website for the next country I was to visit. For the record, I was never really intimidated by the threat of catching some tropical disease. The scary part for me was always how I was going to pay for all the shots and medicine I needed just to go on one of the trips. The cost of vaccinations was often staggering.

Over the years, and on almost all my visits to foreign countries, I stayed relatively healthy, and I am thankful to have never been taken to an emergency room or admitted to a hospital. That said, I have had my share of bowel issues in several countries. My advice to first-time short-term mission trip team members was always, "I take Exlax and Immodium at the same time and let them battle it out." And, "diarrhea can be your best friend." I always had a full arsenal of bathroom jokes to produce groans from my team members.

I got really sick on my second trip to the Dominican Republic as a faculty member for their National Youth Conference and spent an entire night bowing before the porcelain throne while begging God to just take my life as a martyr. The next day, my fellow Americans quarantined me for 24 hours to recover and keep my microbes to myself. Most of my stomach issues on mission trips have been gifts from the Christian Home for displaced children outside of San Luis Potosí in Mexico. One year after having thought I had escaped Montezuma's Revenge and returned to the States, I suffered for a full week of almost constant diarrhea. My primary care physician wanted me to collect and bring back a specimen. Since I wasn't up for trying to bag a poop geyser, I decided to play my "get a second opinion" card. It was my friend Dr. Frank who introduced me to what would become a familiar friend on many mission trips: an antibiotic called Ciprofloxacin. I figured if Cipro could battle anthrax for our troops, it could probably deal with anything I might encounter on future trips to foreign lands.

In addition to my own health concerns on trips, I always had to fulfill my role as a leader and keep a watchful eye on my team members. I had to nurse people through various viruses, scorpion bites, altitude sickness, lice, bed bugs, wasp stings, muscle pulls, heat exhaustion and dehydration. I held my youngest daughter Jenna's hair as she lost her cookies in an airplane barf bag while flying somewhere over Brazil on our way to Paraguay and I should have been nominated as "Father of the Century" for helping my oldest daughter Maressa transition into womanhood on her first mission trip to St. Vincent. Note: my award would be rescinded when it was learned I racked up a $500 phone bill that week so Maressa could get the help she REALLY needed by talking to her mom. I thought about buying her a custom T-shirt which read, "I became a woman on a mission trip to St. Vincent" but apparently women don't like to be recognized for such accomplishments. I feel incredibly blessed for the fact that in all the years I've been leading trips no one has ever been seriously injured or become so ill as to have to return early from a trip. I attribute this to the dozens of people back home who always prayed for me and their friends and family who served with me on these trips.

Speaking of prayer, it would surprise no one to learn the number one prayer requests shared by all team members preparing for trips is safety. I keep waiting for a team member to list "adventure" as a thing to have folks praying for us, but it has never happened. Three of the scariest "adventures" I've encountered on my foreign trips all happened in what should have been one of my safest assignments. At the Christian Home in San Luis Potosí, where 20-30 children live, our team members have one mission: "To love and care for the children of the home and make our time with them the best week of their summer." These are children whose parents, for whatever reasons, could no longer provide for their physical and emotional needs. Juan and Salena, who were once children living at the home, serve as mom and dad to a very large family of kids. The way this family did life and the way they spread joy and love to me and my teams over the years made this one of my favorite places in the world to visit.

A tradition on our trip to the Christian Home in San Luis was to take the children from the home to a fun filled and "all the tacos you can eat" evening at the State Fair, la feira. Each of our team members would be assigned two to three children and be equipped with enough money to allow the children to experience all the things you think of at a fair: rides, attractions, Midway games and fried everything. Juan and Selena loaded us all up in the family vehicles and made sure we all entered the fair safely. Once in, they told us we would all reconnect for dinner at Tacos las Volcanoes and then they kind of just disappeared. The excitement of the children coupled with our own enthusiasm to show the kids the night of their lives caused us all to toss caution into the wind. It never occurred to us we were the only white people among tens of thousands of Mexicans AND we were holding hands with and giving piggyback rides to the CUTEST kids in the entire country. Less than fifteen minutes into our oblivious bliss, the military style police decked in camouflage uniforms and toting assault rifles built a perimeter around us and they weren't smiling. Who could blame them? They must have been thinking, "What are these people doing with our kids?" What made matters worse was Juan and Salena were nowhere to be found, and finding them on this massive site wasn't going to be an option now that we were surrounded. None of our team members spoke any Spanish, and I couldn't see how I was going to avoid spending the night in a Mexican jail. As tensions grew and their protective perimeter shrank, we finally saw one of the teens from the home who had stayed just close enough to our group to talk to the police and explain who we were and why we were with the children. I breathed a sigh of relief and we went on to have a magical evening with the kids. And the tacos were off the charts!

Another year at the Christian Home in San Luis, I had a young child on each arm as we navigated through a crowd of people not far from the entrance to the fair. It was opening night and apparently the masses had come out to take advantage of the low-price fair entrance to see one the country's most popular boy bands. Before I knew what was happening, the children and I were completely surrounded by a pushing and shoving mob making their way to the grandstand for the free concert. I was being pushed so hard in my back it was all I could do to remain standing. The children, who were waist high and suffocating in the closing walls of humanity, were visually shaken with the look of death on their faces. I was firmly convinced that if I could not keep my footing we would easily be trampled to death. My teammate John was a few feet ahead of me and in the same unbreakable sea of people trying to protect his two children as well. John was the biggest guy at the fair. He was as big as an NFL linebacker, and I'll never forget the fear in his eyes and the panic in his voice as he shouted back to me, "This is not good. I don't like this!" The swell of people was suffocating, and as I dug my heels into the pavement to keep from getting myself and my young charges trampled, I knew I had to plot our escape. After about fifteen minutes of high anxiety, I moved slightly to my right into an area where artisans were selling their wares from kiosks. Suddenly the throngs of people divided on our left and on our right. I looked ahead to find my linebacker friend John had made the same move. It was like we had swum through a sea of bodies and then waded ashore on a peninsula as the waters of people parted on either side of us. After settling there in the middle of the chaos for a few minutes, the crowds eventually died down and we made our way safely to another part of the fair. Both of my hands were numb after the children held on so tight for so long.

Being surrounded by Mexican police with assault rifles and being nearly trampled to death at to a concert I wasn't even trying to attend, were not my last adventures in San Luis Potosí. One year as the team was heading to the airport on our way back to the States I decided, along with one of our teen guys, to "take one for the team" by volunteering to ride in the back of Juan's pickup truck on top of all our suitcases while the rest of the team crammed into the family van. For some reason that day, a man named Richard, the father of one of our teens, was driving the pickup truck and for some other reason, like maybe divine providence, the much newer and faster van decided to allow us to lead the caravan to the airport. About halfway to the airport, our pickup truck backfired and huge flames shot out from under the truck. Knowing something was wrong, Richard quickly pulled off the side of the road and quickly jumped out of the cab and shouted for me and his son to jump off and move away from the truck. The team van following us parked on the shoulder at a safe distance from the truck. Apparently, the fireball under the truck was so frightening it brought tears to the eyes of our team members who watched in horror from the van behind us as they feared for our lives. What I couldn't see had caused me to think I was in store for another routine broken down vehicle on a mission trip. In reality, the experience was something far more potentially dangerous.

A few years later I experienced one of my more frightening experiences abroad. In all my foreign travels I have never been able to sleep on a plane. I tried everything and finally resigned myself to the fact my body would just have to adjust in whatever country and time zone I landed in. On my first trip to the continent of Africa, and after a night with no sleep and a several-hour layover in Paris, I was running on fumes when we finally arrived at the airport in Abidjan in the Ivory Coast. Another Crooked River guy, Damon, who grew up in the same small town and small church as I had, met us at the airport. Like me, Damon had developed a heart for the world at the Crocker Christian Church and Ozark Christian College, and was serving, along with his wife Julie, as a missionary at a church and HIV Clinic in the Ivory Coast. We threw our gear on top of the Land Rover and began our four-hour journey from Abidjan to Abengourou. The first leg of our journey offered paved roads and amazing sights for someone who had never visited any part of Africa before. When I did feel like I was getting sleepy I reminded myself to wait until bedtime so my sleep schedule could match Ivory Coast time. The second half of our journey, though, had us driving over dirt roads riddled with potholes we had to avoid like landmines. Like any period of struggle after a period of peace, this part seemed to take forever. I remember finally getting out of the Land Rover and giving Damon's wife, Julie, a hug while apologizing for being so sweaty. She smiled and said, "Don't worry about it, we're used to giving and getting sweaty hugs here." We had an amazing meal and spent some time with Damon and Julie's loveable children – they had a family of teenagers, toddlers, and everything in between – before finally being driven a short distance to our bunkhouses. After unpacking and getting my bearings I climbed up on a metal-framed and squeaky bunk bed. I was sound asleep almost instantly.

After about eight hours of the deepest sleep I have ever experienced, I heard what sounded like primal chanting right outside my window. The chanting seemed to be getting louder, and in my drowsy and "not sure where in the world I am right now" state, I could have sworn I was about to be abducted by a tribe of hostile people who would take me further into the jungle and burn me at the stake. In the moment I couldn't tell if I was asleep or awake, but the noise sent a paralyzing fear up and down my body; I could not move. Turns out I was so sleep deprived I had forgotten I was in a city, not a jungle, and the chants I heard were the prayers of Muslims being broadcast over a load speaker from the mosque in the center of the town not far from where we were staying. In the days that followed, the once frightening chants became a soothing wakeup call every morning I was in in the Ivory Coast.

Toward the end of my time in Abengourou, Damon took the guys in our group to pray for a man who had cut himself on the leg with a machete. The smell of urine and feces was overpowering in the one-room shack where the man was staying, and it was all I could do to hang in and pray for this dirt poor and desperate man. He had developed gangrene, we learned, and his leg needed to be amputated. As we prayed for this dear and humble man who had the misfortune of not having access to proper care for his wound, the women on our team sat at the bedside of a woman as she passed away from AIDS. When we returned to the States, we learned the man with gangrene had also died after his amputation.

One of the scariest sights I've ever witnessed while serving abroad happened in Managua, Nicaragua. Through our local church contacts, we learned of an entire community living right on the edges of the city dump. The people were picking off the trash piles to provide for their families. Their homes and clothing were the worst I had ever seen or would ever see in any place in the world. Even the government felt for these poorest of poor people, and though they did not offer anything in the way of manpower or supplies, they supported our efforts by allowing us to host a medical clinic and "day spa" at one of their buildings not far from the community. Our hosts warned our doctors and nurses that malnutrition, parasites, and lice would be prominent in almost every patient they would attend to. I will never forget climbing into the back of a truck with a few team members for my first tour of the Managua City Dump. We drove through a maze of burning and foul-smelling rubbish piles which towered ten feet high on both sides of the truck. The putrid smells, smoke, dust, and toxic fumes encompassing the truck caused me to gag as I quickly pulled the neck of my shirt up to my forehead to cover my eyes, nose, and mouth. Everywhere I looked I saw burning piles of trash. Ahead of us another truck filled with young men was weaving through the trash mountains. Those in the back of their truck kept pointing at us and laughing. I thought for sure at any minute they were going to stop and rob us inside their protected and burning labyrinth. After about five minutes of the tour through what felt like hell, I banged on the top of the cab with my fist and then screamed through the rolled-up window on the driver's side, "Get us out of here!" We quickly returned to a government building on the outskirts of the dump, where I watched my team give "hose showers", lice treatments, bathrobes, and a set of clean clothes and flip flops to the dirtiest and most desperate children I have ever seen. The team encouraged me to participate and as I washed the dirt-caked feet of a young man and poured clean and cold water from a hose over his head rinsing off the de-lice shampoo he giggled in pure delight. Our Crooked River Mission Team performed this same loving act to dozens of kids at our day spa for kids at the dump in Managua.

Travel, health, and safety issues were not the only things I had to persevere through on foreign trips. Having grown up eating squirrel, rabbit, and frog, one would think I'd be naturally inclined to enjoy pretty much anything put in front of me; one would be wrong. I grew up a picky eater infamous for his refusal to try new foods. New food experiences – central to any engagement with foreign cultures – turned out to be a significant challenge for me. Many would consider my diet as a kid to be primitive (which I guess it was) but it was consistent. As a family we never ate seafood. We only ate the fish we caught on the Crooked River. I grew up having never even heard of sushi and other such things which are staples in other countries. In fact, I can remember our family eating rice only rarely, if ever at all. We were a bland, meat and potatoes kind of family. I learned, however, as part of my training for foreign work, to eat whatever was placed in front of me with gratitude, and to do other-wise would be to insult our host, who was likely offering the very best they had to offer.

The core value of "eat what is offered" was tested early when, on my first foreign trip, I found myself in a rainforest village on the border of the Dominican Republic and Haiti. Our gracious Dominican hosts were cooking something in a big pot over an open fire but started the course by offering me a slice of the best pineapple I had ever tasted. Then, after hearing someone mention we were having chicken, I breathed a sigh of relief and thought, "The eat what is offered" rule will be easily obeyed for this meal." Our guests, in humble fashion, motioned me up to the front of the line. What could go wrong? I approached the boiling pot of chicken and grabbed a utensil and began stirring the meat around, looking for a familiar piece. I couldn't find anything that resembled a piece of American chicken. Suddenly I felt all this pressure to make a choice. The line of people behind me was growing impatient. I could hear them, under their breaths saying, "C'mon Mr. Picky Eater, just choose something, we're starving to death back here." With great anxiety I finally snagged what I thought looked like a safe choice: a chicken leg. As I pulled it out, I was surprised to see the claw still attached. I held my chicken leg with claw plate out in front of my body like hoisting a trophy to the roar, applause, and delight of the crowd. I later learned the significance of my selection: I, an honored guest, had chosen an honored piece of the chicken. All I could think about was plucking chickens back in Missouri. I ate the entire piece, minus the claw, along with some rice and beans and plantains. It was a delicious meal, and I could not have been more thankful to those would had provided and prepared it for me.

It's not just the food which challenges the missionary traveler, but the drinks as well. Americans believe we are the only country in the world with safe drinking water, which is funny because the water where I live in the DC suburbs tastes so bad we drink, you guessed it, bottled water, and when we've had guests from other countries stay in our home we tell them, "Don't drink the water from the tap." On my first visit to the Philippines, where I was planning to visit my sponsored child, Kristen Joy with the Christian non-profit Food for the Hungry we were told many of the children living in a village where our church sponsored children were getting deathly ill and missing school because they were drinking contaminated water. With help from Food for the Hungry, we found an American company who made portable water filters which made use of five-gallon water buckets and were used around the world with great success. Our church mission team held fund raisers and purchased dozens of these water filters to give away in and around a small village called Matictic. We carefully drilled holes in the plastic buckets and then divided into teams to give the new water drinking systems to those living in extreme poverty. But there was an unforeseen wrinkle.

Our Filipino hosts from Food for the Hungry told us the people would not be convinced our water filters would provide clean drinking water until we drank from it ourselves. It made sense. I mean, if people from another country came to your house with a bucket and a weird looking contraption you had never seen hanging from it and then, through a translator, told you how you could fill the bucket from any source of water you could find and drink it without worry, you would probably say something like, "I'm going to need to see YOU drink it first." Or as they say in Missouri where I'm from, "Show me." Personally, I was not prepared for this wrinkle in what had been, up to that time, a pretty tame foreign trip experience, but I was the leader of this team and leaders have to lead by example. I took a tin can and walked over to an overflowing mud puddle in the middle of the dirt road. The water's color was on the dark side of gray as I poured it from the can into an orange bucket. As I filled the bucket, I imagined what was in the water: mosquito larvae, animal urine and poop, fuel, and God only knows what else. I carried the bucket of filthy water to the sponsored family's house, a simple bamboo structure with a blue tarp roof held down by old tires thrown on the top. By now a crowd of neighbors had gathered. They had watched me fill my bucket with the dirtiest water on the planet and now they had come to watch the freak show. I felt like a magician as I made everyone look into the bucket at the dirty water. I asked my lovely assistant for a clean glass. I opened the tap as the fresh, crystal clear water filled the cup. I heard the gasps of the crowd as I displayed the clear water and then, just before I knocked it back, prayed the fastest and most desperate silent prayer I had ever prayed. "Dear God, I don't know who the people are who made this water filter, but I pray to you they didn't have a bad day when they made this one." For dramatic effect, on all my water demos that week, I never simply sipped or took a small drink of the water. I killed it. I drank it all at once and finished it off with a satisfied, refreshed *aahhh!* like someone in a beverage commercial. The crowd went wild, and then, to ensure our water system would be used after we left, we invited the adults living in the community to drink the water first and then the children. After everyone had drunk, we taught them how to flush the filters to keep the water pressure flowing at a good speed and then we went to the next neighborhood for a new demo. I did these in-home water tastings for a couple days that week and other than a pesky cough which hung around with me the whole summer, I returned to the States and suffered no ill effects from drinking the dirtiest water in the world.

Another water issue bubbled up when I was in Paraguay, only this time it was what the locals were putting in the water. As part of our orientation, my good friend Billy, who was serving as a church planter in Paraguay, warned our team about how it was a custom for the people there to offer their guests a caffeine-rich infused drink called *mate* (the "e" on the end is pronounced like a long "a" in English: MAH-tay) or *chimarrão*. It is prepared by steeping dried leaves of yerba mate in hot water and is served in a mug with a built-in stainless-steel straw. Everyone drinks mate in Paraguay. It's like Starbucks. I can remember watching our host pick what looked, to me, like weeds alongside the road throughout the day only to learn it would be for the mate our team would "enjoy" later that night at a Bible study small group in his house. In advance of our "Mate "Partay" we received a debriefing from missionary Billy. He said, "They'll probably offer you guys mate, which tastes like bad tea, but you have to drink it because it's their way of showing you guys respect." And then he said something which put all of us Americans who washed our hands every twenty minutes on foreign fields with sanitizing wipes into a state of horror. He said, "And the worst part is you don't get your own cup of *mate*. The whole group drinks from the same straw in the same cup as they pass it around the circle." And so, like those preparing to face the firing squad, our team headed to the "Mate Partay House." Billy dropped us off, waved goodbye, and said, "Good luck." As our team sat in a circle in a medium sized living room, the *mate* mug began making the rounds in clockwise fashion. I was to be the first American in the circle to drink. As the *mate* mug moved around the circle it came to within two people of me...my body clinched as I prepared for the hemlock. And then, for reasons only God Himself knows, the mug reversed and stayed within the semi-circle of the locals. Once again my life had been saved. Later in the week when our team had a tour day, I bought a *mate* mug fridge magnet which I promptly placed on my refrigerator when I returned home.

I managed to survive all of my worldwide food and drink adventures, but the closest I believe I came to death was picking up pizzas in Taipei, Taiwan. From day one our team had fully embraced the culture and particularly the food. Growing up, the closest I ever came to seafood was the freshwater fish we caught on the Crooked River which doesn't resemble the often strong and ocean taste of seafood, but in Taiwan, I made up for lost time. The offerings, especially for dinner, were usually a mix of several different vegetables, fish, and miscellaneous seafood offerings, and I felt I was better off just eating it without asking for the particulars of what it was. At one of our dinners, we were told our host wanted to honor his guests by offering the most precious piece of food on the table: the fish eyeball. Fortunately for me, team member Emory stepped up to the plate that night and took the "honor" for our team.

At the end of our week of serving in Taiwan, our missionary host, Scott (a fellow Ozark Christian College alum) praised our team for not only embracing the culture but for even choosing local food when more familiar Western fare was readily available at a nearby mall. He was very impressed and wanted to reward us by ordering pizzas for the group from the Pizza Hut in Taipei. This was very exciting for me, and I quickly volunteered to help Scott pick up the pizzas for our group and his family. As Scott and I made our way down the elevator from the high-rise apartment I was sure we would take the family van to the local Pizza Hut. Instead, Scott took me outside his apartment complex to a parking area where we found his moped. The thought of riding on the back of a moped through the busy streets of Taipei was just the type of adventure I was seeking to finish another great week of serving in a foreign country, and the weaving in and out of traffic in one of the largest cities in the world was a thrill and pure joy. More than once, though, I had to grab and grip Scott around his waist or dig my fingers into his back just to keep my balance and stay on the moped. After our "fast and furious" ride through downtown Taipei, we got to the Pizza Hut, and as I saw our stack of pizza boxes, it suddenly occurred to me we had no basket or carrier in the front or the back of the moped and there wasn't enough room on it for me to put the boxes between me and Scott. I sheepishly asked Scott, "So, what's the plan for carrying these back to your apartment?" Without a care or concern for my life he quickly answered, "You'll have to balance them in both of your arms off the sides of the moped." I wanted to reply, "Awesome but...Those claw marks on your sides and back are from when I almost died just getting here and that was without me trying to balance four pizza boxes in both arms. Maybe we should have rethought the whole moped thing... and by the way, can't they just deliver these?" But we were two men on a food gathering mission from God, and if it cost us our lives, so be it. My greatest fear, though, was not death itself but death on foreign soil, as an American missionary surrounded by Pizza Hut boxes. There could be no greater shame. I could visualize the headlines on the front pages of newspapers all over the world: **"Renowned American Missionary Pastor Chino dies in Taipei moped accident. Body covered in Pizza Hut Boxes."** My home church back in Crocker, Missouri would rescind my ordination and my parents, in shame, would have to relocate. My famed missionary sending school, Ozark Christian College, would conveniently lose all records I had ever attended the school. My mission trip teammates, for whom I died to get the only American food they would have eaten all week, would have to change their identities and go through years of grief and guilt counseling. Fortunately, Scott and I made it back to the apartment, and when I placed those pizzas on the table, I knew I had risked everything and made the ultimate sacrifice. I can only hope my experience is retold among the stories of great men and women who, at the risk of their very lives, gave it all for the good of others.

The end of most float trips I took as a boy on the Crooked River resulted in a nice stringer of fish and a boatload of new memories to last a lifetime. That's not to say the trips didn't come with their share of intense moments, challenges, twists and turns, and some aches and pains along the way. But it was always worth it. In similar ways, the experiences of nearly being trampled to death, burned alive in the back of a truck and locked in a Mexican jail were worth the pure joy of riding to a stop at the apex on a Ferris Wheel with two young orphaned girls from Mexico at a state fair, their dark eyes looking across the swaying car at me against the backdrop of green, yellow, and red flashing lights from the midway a hundred feet below.

The hellish ride through the burning trash piles at the Managua City Dump and having all our gear confiscated at the airport was worth the thousands of patients my team treated at mobile clinics over the years and the personal touch I had at the Managua trash dump washing a young boy's feet, picking through his hair for lice and sending him home with a new shirt, shorts, and a pair of flip flops.

The helpless feeling I had of trying to get my oldest daughter through her first period and mission trip was worth watching how she loved and cared for the beautiful island children of St. Vincent in spite of how she was feeling.

Holding my youngest daughter's hair while she vomited in a barf bag was worth seeing her serve children and give away her entire toy collection at a church sponsored carnival in Paraguay. Getting to see the most spectacular vista I have ever witnessed in creation, The Iguacu Falls, was a nice bonus as well.

The faith testing water tasting demos I did in the rural villages of the Philippines was worth what remains today my greatest cross-cultural experience ever: visiting the young girl, Kristen Joy, whom my family and I sponsored through Food for the Hungry. I will never forget when this young girl grabbed my hand and led me down a muddy path to her bamboo, dirt floor and two-room shack where she lived with her mom and dad and three siblings. I will never forget offering them simple and practical gifts, praying for their family and then leaving with the thought that they had just enriched my life in ways I had never experienced.

Eating strange foods, getting stuck on the side of the road, putting my body through the torture of long flights and bumpy roads was worth meeting the most joyful, humble, and loving people in the world, people who touched my life in ways I struggle to find words to describe. No matter where I was in the world, I always learned more than I taught and received more than I gave. And just like the Crooked River taught me so many valuable lessons, the many experiences and relationships I have built with others all over the world have given me an honorary PhD in perseverance and how life was meant to be lived.

CHAPTER SEVEN:
SOAKING UP EVIL

I believe like a child that suffering will be healed and made up for, that all the humiliating absurdity of human contradictions will vanish like a pitiful mirage, like the despicable fabrication of the impotent and infinitely small Euclidean mind of man, that in the world's finale, at the moment of eternal harmony, something so precious will come to pass that it will suffice for all hearts, for the comforting of all resentments, for the atonement of all the crimes of humanity, of all the blood that they've shed; that it will make it not only possible to forgive but to justify all that has happened.
-Fyodor Dostoevsky, *The Brothers Karamazov*, 1880

Though the Gasconade bends its way over and back on its quest through the Ozark Mountains, it never once breaks. This is true, as well, of the Crooked River People who built their lives on the river. One doesn't become a Crooked River Person by simply living near the water's edge. You have to travel the river. You have to get knocked out of the boat a time or two. You have to get one of those "blisters on your back" sunburns because you ignored warnings to leave your shirt on. You have to get caught in a downpour because you "poo-pooed" the weather forecast. You have to be covered with mosquito bites and slap a few cottonmouths over the head with a boat paddle. You have to fish all day and return home without catching a fish or without getting a bite before the river of perseverance shapes your character. It's a process which can take years, but, just as the Crooked River is shaped by its arduously winding journey through the Ozarks, this river of perseverance shapes your character.

As a kid, I didn't respond very well to swift waters or what you might call "character developing life crisis moments." Once, I was visiting with my relatives on my uncle's farm, and my cousin from the city who thought she could ride a country horse suddenly lost all control of the animal. It began galloping like it was on fire and ran under an apple tree with low hanging limbs. I remember hearing the thud of my cousin's body falling off the horse and hitting the hard Missouri dirt from about fifty yards away. In that moment it seemed like everyone except me knew what to do. Some ran for the house to get the adults. Others raced over to provide aid to my cousin. I did nothing. Eventually, the adults arrived and my bloodied and bruised cousin was taken to the hospital with broken ribs. As everyone else did their part to get my cousin the care she needed, I remember standing there, frozen, and thinking selfishly, "I was supposed to ride the horse next."

A few years later, I was invited by a friend to attend a St. Louis Cardinals baseball game, which was a big deal for a poor, Crooked River Kid. The drive seemed to last forever as I clutched my baseball mitt and imagined myself snagging a prized foul ball. About thirty minutes from the ballpark, our car was suddenly side swiped on Interstate 44, leading to a multi-car accident which involved fatalities. I remember watching as multiple ambulances arrived and police cars shut down the highway. I sat in a grassy area safe from the road as injured and screaming victims were loaded onto mats and into ambulances and driven to local hospitals. It remains today the most horrific traffic accident I have ever witnessed. While there probably wasn't much a young man like me could have done to make things better, I remember, again selfishly, having to be delayed over an hour waiting for the accident scene to clear and missing the first couple innings of the game.

Then came the time when I was sitting in our family living room around supper time and I heard my mom coughing more loudly and more violently than the cough of a winter cold or allergies would merit. I casually strolled in to check on the status of supper and instead saw my mom gripping her throat, gasping for breath. According to family lore, I then slowly walked outside our house to the front porch and with next to no emotion in my voice announced to my dad, "Hey, I think Mom is choking, you might want to go check it out." My dad ran into the kitchen where my mom was desperately trying to clear a piece of chicken lodged in her throat. My dad did his best version of the Heimlich maneuver and helped my mom cough up the perfidious poultry. Upon observing an act which probably saved my mother's life, I responded by going outside to play basketball.

I even proved myself unable to respond well to less-than-lethal family crises. Poor people tend to have utilities in their houses which don't work like they should and never get fixed for lack of resources, and growing up, our family had the worst functioning toilet in the Gasconade River Basin (very prestigious distinction, I know). After every bit of bathroom business that required a flush, we were required to stand by the toilet for what seemed like 10 minutes and shake the handle until the water stopped running into the bowl. If one of us ever forgot to perform this duty, we could hear the yells from as far as a mile away: "Shake the handle!" Today, I know that a simple $5 flapper and chain adjustment inside the tank of the toilet would have solved the problem, but why do that when you can spend the equivalent of three years of your life shaking a toilet handle? We also had more than our fair share of toilet clogs because, let's face it, when six people share the same toilet, shit happens! And in another one of my "Darin is not the guy you want to call on in times of crisis" moments one of our family members clogged the toilet. A Niagara Falls of cascading and contaminated water was about to threaten the very existence of the Brown family, and my mom, in a panic, cried, "Quick, bring me a pan!" Now at this point any normal and intelligent person would have quickly produced a deep pan which could have served to catch or bail a sufficient amount of either yellow or brown water from the soon to be overflowing toilet. But I was neither normal nor intelligent, so I handed my mom the first thing I could find: a centimeter-deep baking sheet. And then I went out to play basketball.

Up until the age of sixteen I had never lost anyone close to me but then on a chilly and foggy fall evening that changed. My best friend called and asked if we had heard my first cousin, Daryl, had been in a car accident. My friend and his dad had been listening on the CB radio and heard police were at the scene. I hung up the phone and reported to my dad what my friend had said. In retrospect, my dad probably should not have taken me with him that night, but sometimes things happen so quickly you just have to jump in the car to go and see what happened. We drove about three miles from our house and came to the accident scene on a very sharp curve on Highway 17 near a building that used to be called "The Sale Barn." My dad parked along the side of the road and together we began moving closer to Daryl's red Ford Mustang. The once-formidable automobile now looked like a balled-up piece of Christmas wrapping paper embedded in a tree. As we approached, we were stopped by the county coroner. He asked us who we were, and when my dad said he was Daryl's uncle, the man sharply replied, "You can't go any further. He's dead and the body is still in the car."

Daryl had not only been my cousin; he was one of my best friends. We had played sports together, went hunting and fishing together, dressed up as cowboys and soldiers together. Now, after a breakup with his girlfriend and one bad night of drinking, he was dead. I remember that night like it was yesterday. I can still feel the cold mist at the accident scene on my skin. I still see the blue and red flashing lights from the police car and ambulance bouncing off the glistening, wet darkness of highway pavement. I can still remember the silent car ride home with my dad. I remember thinking to myself even at sixteen, "I wasn't supposed to be there."

I served as a pallbearer for my cousin's funeral a few days later, but I was too wounded to help anyone else with their grief. In my hurt, I was mad at God for letting my cousin and one of my best friends die.

I had not responded very well to the horseback ride gone bad, a multi-car accident, my mom almost choking to death, and the loss of my cousin Daryl, but the thing about pain and suffering and even evil for that matter, is they will always be around to test us. Though I had failed previous tests, God still believed in me enough to guide a family and an entire community through a grieving process which resulted from the most evil act I have ever encountered.

Jessica and her eleven-year-old son, Jimmy, had been coming to the church in suburban Washington, DC, where I served as the Outreach Pastor for about six months. Though I didn't know them well, I loved seeing how excited they were just to come to the Sunday services we held at a local high school. Jessica was a Crooked River Woman. Through her life, she had endured the rough waters of alcohol abuse, poverty, and failed relationships with men. But by the time I met her, she was on the upswing. She was providing a stable income for herself and Jimmy by holding down a steady job, and more importantly she was getting right with God and becoming more involved in church; she even participated in a mid-week Bible study small group. Jessica could not have been more proud of her handsome and athletic son who loved football and had just started middle school. Life was better for Jessica and Jimmy than it had ever been.

One of the men who had been in Jessica's life did prison time for attempted murder, and upon his release somehow convinced Jessica he had changed and deserved a second chance in her life. Perhaps she still felt a void in her newfound stability, a cold loneliness that maybe a man – especially a familiar one – could replace with warm companion-ship. Perhaps she thought Jimmy needed a father figure, someone to teach him to be the strong, responsible, faithful man she knew he could grow to be. Perhaps she was driven by the mysteries of the human heart. Whatever the reason, she invited this man back into her life and into the home she made for herself and Jimmy. It turned out to be a fatal mistake. One night, when Jimmy was sleeping over at friend's house, the man who Jessica let back into her life promptly took her life while she lay asleep in bed. He could have simply taken her cash and some other property, which seemed to have been his motive. Instead, he picked up young Jimmy at the friend's house later that same day, took him to a secluded area in the woods, and beat him to death. He then drove to North Carolina where he hooked up with another woman and was eventually captured and arrested by the police.

The tragic end of Jessica's and Jimmy's lives hit our church family hard and in two waves. Initially, it was thought that only Jessica had been murdered and Jimmy was still alive. The news media swirled around our church, wondering what we knew about this family and if we had any ideas where Jimmy might be. Our church Youth Pastor, Scott, helped me organize a prayer vigil at Jimmy's school, where we desperately prayed for him to be found alive and safe. The next day, a news reporter promised to connect me to Jessica's brother, Brian, in exchange for a story and any leads we might provide. I was reluctant to make any promises or deals; I believed that if Brian really wanted to contact me, he would. And he did.

We agreed to meet at a corner bakery, and as I was preparing to go into the meeting to console Brian, I could not have felt more inadequate. I was from a small town in Missouri and up to this point in my life I had pretty much failed at any and all kinds of crisis involvement. Now, I was meeting with a man whose sister had been brutally murdered only a couple days before, and his nephew was still missing. I called a couple of close friends and begged them to pray for me before entering the bakery. As Brian and I met, exchanged names and shook hands, he quickly said to me, "I need you to help me plan a memorial service for my sister with a contingency plan for my nephew." I swallowed hard and began to feel my chest tighten. For the next thirty minutes we tried to be strong in each other's presence, but we were just barely holding it together and trying to make sense of the horrific evil which had taken his sister and nephew.

As we sat down and began talking, Brian honestly shared with me his nominal background in Eastern religions and said he didn't want to speculate where his sister was now, after her death. In response, I simply offered what I knew and believed: Jessica had been following Jesus, and the only sense I could make of such a horrific event was to speculate that she was safe in the arms of God even as we were talking. I'm not sure who benefitted more from those words of assurance: Brian or me. (It was probably me.) I then assured him I was connected to other pastors in the area, and I would network with them to provide a building which would be big enough to host Jessica's friends, family and greater community to celebrate her journey through life. After talking for a few minutes, we agreed to plan a church memorial service filled with messages of hope as well as fond memories from the people who were touched by Jessica's life and her story of perseverance. We decided those elements shared by the people she loved would be exactly what she would want us to do. As we got to know each other and as I watched Brian face each and every tragic turn of events with courage, I began referring to him, even in the presence of others, as "Brave Brian."

We weren't very long into our discussion and plans when Brian's cell phone rang. "This is the police calling about Jimmy," he said. "I have to take this." He went outside for only a couple minutes and said upon his return, "They found Jimmy's body. I have to go." We shook hands again and he promised he would be back in touch with me.

After Brian hurried away, there was no longer any need for me to try to stay brave. I completely lost it. I sat back down in a chair, put my head on the table, and began sobbing so uncontrollably I feared another customer might complain and I'd be taken somewhere I didn't want to go. I knew I could not stay in the bakery, so I made my way back to the car and began driving home. I wept to such an extent I almost changed course to the emergency room for fear I was having an emotional break-down and was unsafe to even be driving. The first person to see me when I arrived home was my oldest daughter, Maressa. I knew she could tell that something awful had happened. She escorted me up to my bed and I buried my face in the pillow. Then, suddenly and out of nowhere, a wave of unexpected rage came over me, and I felt much like I did the night I visited my cousin's fatal car accident scene. I called Mark, the Lead Pastor of the church, and started screaming, repeatedly, "They found Jimmy's body in the woods. He's dead. We got the call while I was with Brian planning his sister funeral. I wasn't supposed to be there!" I kept repeating through tears and in an agonized and angry voice, "I wasn't supposed to be there!" It's hard, even for me, to explain what I meant when I said, "I wasn't supposed to be there." Maybe it was my past failures in times of crisis resurfacing. Maybe it was fear. Maybe it was the voice of childlike innocence when it encounters overwhelming evil. I still don't know why I said it.

My loving wife, lead pastor Mark and his wife Barbara all came to my side right when I needed them, and after a couple of days I began to get better. Once the news of Jimmy's death hit the airwaves, it seemed like every news outlet in the DC area had somehow gotten ahold of my cell phone number and were calling me for a story. Initially I gave them nothing, but eventually I gave them the details of the memorial service and requested they stay away and allow the family and community a safe place to grieve and heal. The four weeks between Jessica and Jimmy's deaths and the memorial service allowed the waters to calm while the news cycled to other stories. Brian, who had returned to be with his family on the West coast, communicated with me concerning the plans for the dual memorial services.

When I was ordained as a minister in a small country church near the Crooked River, I never imagined I would preside over a memorial service for a double homicide twenty minutes outside what some regard as the most powerful city in the world. As the time for the memorial service got close, I remember praying over and over again, "God, please don't let this thing get bigger than me and the strength you will provide." It was a prayer God answered immediately. A perfect church building large enough for the expected crowd became available. Some of the pastors from the church had known Jessica when she was struggling financially and had even helped her get settled in her first place by providing household essentials. A group of women from the same church also offered to help provide and set up a lunch for friends and family following the service. Some of Jessica's coworkers and friends offered to give eulogies along with some teachers from Jimmy's school. Two ladies from our own church found papers Jimmy had completed in his own writing during his time in our children's church program expressing his own childlike faith in Jesus and they asked to share Jimmy's own words concerning his trust in Christ. One of the best male vocalists I have ever heard offered to sing a song to help the community heal. Looking back, I can see how God was surrounding me and the family and all of Jessica and Jimmy's friends with his comfort and care.

As the memorial service started, I walked up the blue carpeted stairs to the stage and made my way to the podium. Before I spoke, I asked God one more time to help me say words which would somehow comfort all those who had gathered, all those who sought healing from the senseless act of evil which had taken two beloved people. With a fairly long list of speakers and prayers and scriptures to be read, I kept my comments short; I chose rather to provide a platform and to defer to those who knew Jessica and Jimmy way better than I did. I fought back tears as I saw a group of young men from Jimmy's football team sitting in the middle of the crowded room. I gathered myself and I shared with the congregated mourners how our grief and sense of loss were needed and appropriate and in proportion to the amount of love we had for and shared with Jessica and Jimmy. I shared a short story of a father who carried his young son through an unexpected rainstorm on a camping trip while holding him tight and all the while whispering in his ear over and over again, "I got you buddy. It's going to be alright. We're going to make it." The story ended with the father and son making it back to the cabin and being greeted by a sun-filled sky. I told the crowd how I believed God had done those same things for Jessica and Jimmy even in the midst of the cruelty they experienced and how he wanted to do the same for us in the midst of our loss and grief.

Jessica's brother, Brave Brian, spoke last and shared his gratitude for all who had gathered and reminded us of Jessica's Crooked River journey and Jimmy's fun-loving personality. A slide show of pictures set to music followed, and then the host pastor closed the service with a prayer in which he noted how we had grieved for and remembered well two very special people who would be missed dearly.

As the years have passed, the memory of Jessica and Jimmy has stayed with me. I still think about them and those difficult days following their deaths. The house where Jessica's life was taken is less than three miles from my house, and almost every time I drive near her neighborhood, I think about her and Jimmy. If I'm being honest, I probably should have gotten some counseling for myself in the wake of all that happened. To this day I hardly ever watch the news or find any desire to know more about the latest school shooting or anything related to the taking of innocent lives by evil people. Still, I cannot escape the fact of God placing me – and you, too – on a fallen planet where we all encounter evil and brokenness in various forms throughout our lives. In fact, more days than not, I feel like a helpless kid trying to bail shit water from an overflowing toilet using a centimeter-deep baking sheet while crying out to God or whoever else will listen, "I'm not supposed to be here." Maybe you can relate.

In his book, *The Jesus I Never Knew,* author Philip Yancey writes of Jesus' crucifixion and its impact on a fallen, broken, and evil world. Quoting M. Scott Peck who, in turn, is quoting a battle-tested, Crooked River Priest, Yancey writes the following:

> "There are dozens of ways to deal with evil and several ways to conquer it. All of them are facets of the truth that the only way to conquer evil is to let it be smothered within a willing, living human being. When it is absorbed there, like blood in a sponge or a spear into one's heart, it loses its power and goes no further. The healing of evil (scientifically or otherwise) can be accomplished only by the love of individuals. A willing sacrifice is required...I do not know how this occurs, but I know it does. Whenever this happens there is a slight shift in the balance of power in the world."

Thinking back about my role in Jessica and Jimmy's memorial service and the healing which took place, and in many ways is still taking place, I have come to realize God put me right where He needed me. I *was* supposed to be there. It just took a lot of trips down the Crooked River to get me there.

CHAPTER EIGHT:
YOU GOTTA GO TO WORK

"Sometimes I feel like giving up, but I just can't. It isn't in my blood."
-Shawn Mendes, "In My Blood," 2018

A common caricature of the Missouri Hillbilly features a sleepy, lazy, unshaved, bib overall wearing man sitting on the front porch of a barely standing shack he calls home. He's wearing a dirty and floppy hat which covers half of his face and sitting next to him is an equally uninspired bloodhound whose long ears dangle off the side of the gray rotted, wood porch. In the hillbilly's lap sits a jug of moonshine and near his hip lies a spittoon. In all the years I grew up in Missouri, I never met this guy or anyone who even closely resembled him.

By contrast, my dad worked in a tire shop in conditions which easily could've qualified for a segment on the television show *Dirty Jobs*. Every day he got up before sunrise, ate a quick breakfast, drank a cup of coffee, and drove ten miles from Crocker to Dixon. More than just fixing flats or installing new tires, my dad's job was to recap old tires. This required using tools to lathe and buff old and worn out tires and then wrapping them with new sheets of rubber before placing them in a scorching hot molding machine. The tire shop was freezing cold in the winter and insufferably hot in the summer. My dad came home every night at exactly the same time covered in black dirt and rubber particles. He washed his hands, ate dinner, took a bath, watched TV, interacted with us kids as much as he could and went to bed. He did this for more than fifteen years and made $100 a week, and I can never remember him missing a day of work. He never called in sick, took a mental health day, or overslept. My dad was the Cal Ripken, Jr, of tire shop guys. I watched this unfold as a child and it marked me.

Meanwhile, my mom worked at home, raising me and my three siblings. She did all the things stay at home moms do, but back then those things were harder. She changed and washed cloth diapers through thousands of messes. She washed our clothes and hung them out on a clothesline. Because we were poor, she had to grocery shop carefully and make meals stretch out longer. In what should be counted as a modern-day miracle, she fed four of us kids with one can of soup. She cooked fantastic meals, cleaned everything in sight, made beds, folded clothes, cleaned up vomit, massaged sore ankles with rubbing alcohol way past everyone's bedtime, and prayed like a mad monk for her four kids as they navigated adolescence. She picked buckshot out of rabbit butts, threw wood in the heat stove, solved the family pinworm crisis, and managed the family finances. My mom saved up for Christmas and saved the holiday for us every year. And while I have memories of her insisting that we grow up by helping around the house, I have none of her complaining or desiring a life other than the one she had. When my youngest brother, Landis, started kindergarten, my mom retired from being a stay at home mom and became a cook at our local school. Still, her work at the school didn't provide much relief from meeting the needs of her husband and children as she continued to carry a heavy load of domestic responsibilities even while holding a fulltime job. I've never met a harder working woman than my mom.

My parents were typical of the many moms and dads who both grew up and raised their own families near the Crooked River. My whole life was a front row seat to the lives of hard-working folks who did whatever it took to provide for their families. They took pride in their professions and often had whispered, even critical, conversations about those who were able-bodied but chose not to work and instead lived on welfare.

With this Protestant work ethic in our blood and culture, it wasn't surprising my parents encouraged all of us kids to start working, even if it was something small, in our early teens. My dad helped me land my first job which was to mow a small patch of grass in the front of his cousin's Delano gas station. Honestly there wasn't much grass to mow, but because it formed a gully that was too steep for his riding lawn mower, I was charged to mow it once a week with a push mower. I remember loading the family push mower into the bed of my dad's truck and then heading to my first real job. By this time, my dad was working as a butcher at a local grocery store, but still kept his Cal Ripken streak of unmissed workdays intact while I was preparing to begin my own "never miss a day of work" perseverance record. The plan was for him to drop me off at the gas station and then, after I completed the job, I would walk a mile and a half home and dad would pick up the mower on his way home from work.

As we drove to the gas station, I remember feeling like a real man on my way to my first real job. Once we arrived, we quickly offloaded the mower and I adjusted the throttle at the handle like my dad had taught me and pulled the start rope. In a rare and glorified moment, the mower started on the first pull. Over the roar of the motor and ascending dust and debris encompassing me, I gave my dad the thumbs up sign that I was good to go. As he got into his truck and headed to work, I just knew it was a proud moment for him as a father. I carefully positioned my feet to descend the gully so as not to let the mower get away from me and to ensure I would not slip. Bad things can happen when steep hills and lawn mowers share the same real estate, and I had always heard of some poor soul who had his feet chopped off from having slipped while mowing grass with a push lawn mower down a steep hill. As I began mowing the thick grass, I could hear chunks of gravel and pieces of glass from broken beer bottles ricocheting off the mower's blades. Big chunks of grass were spewing out from the side of the mower and my testosterone levels were soaring. I was doing it! I was working my first job! My mind began to imagine how I would spend the $2.00 I was earning for my landscaping prowess, and in a moment I dreamt of owning my own company someday and sitting in an air-conditioned office while people who worked for me mowed gullies at gas stations. Then it happened. As I mowed over a thick clump of grass the mower stalled, sputtered, and then completely stopped. My first real job had come to an abrupt end after only five minutes of work.

For the next hour I did everything I knew to get the mower started again. There would be no quitting in this Crooked River Lawn Mowing Boy! I must have pulled the starting rope a hundred times or more, as evidenced by the blisters between each of my fingers on both of my hands. The lawn mower never started, and my first job ended in failure. With my head held low I kicked the same rock down a dirt road all the way back to my house, and by the time we had enough money to fix the lawn mower someone else had taken my job. I had been essentially "fired" from my first job.

It wasn't long after my failed lawn mowing gig I secured a summer job as a maintenance worker for the City of Crocker. I worked with a crew of six other guys, some of whom were high school students like me. We labored in the hot summer sun doing projects like road repairs, street and sidewalk sweeping, painting fire hydrants, weed trimming, and mowing grass with lawn mowers which actually worked.

The summer had been pretty uneventful until that fateful morning when my boss commanded, "Hey boys, load the shovels and bring your gloves. We're going to the sewer plant." Those are words no one ever wants to hear, but when you're young and stupid and earning minimum wage, you do as you're told. In a flash, we were sitting in the back of an old army truck headed to the city's Water Treatment Facility, AKA the sewer plant. The truck was backed up to a parcel of ground about the size of half a basketball court, and we were instructed to start digging up the "dirt" and loading in on the truck.

The plot of ground was gray on the top with zigzagging cracks all across the surface, and although it was a little crusty on the top, it was soft to the shovel and came up without much effort. Beneath the gray top layer was a darker moist layer, which was what we would be standing and sitting on when we got back in the truck. Once we had a full "load" we climbed up on top of the mountain we had created and stuck our shovels in the dirt like proud soldiers who had just conquered an enemy hill. Someone asked, "Where are we taking this?" One of our bosses smiled and replied, "This shit is fertilizer for my garden." It was then we realized we had spent the morning shoveling human waste to put on our boss' garden. We returned and spent the day gathering poop for his potato patch.

Because the waste had decomposed for so long, there was no strong odor to it. In fact, it reminded me of any number of barns I had been in, but still, the thought of it was pretty sickening. Fortunately, the boss' garden wasn't far away, and at the end of the day we hosed our boots and shovels off. We were assured there would be no more jobs at the sewer plant. I can't help but think how, if my friends and I could have been transported to the time of social media, we would have snapped pictures of ourselves and captioned them with clever sayings like:

"Same shit, different day."

"It's a crappy job but someone has to do it."

"Looking out for number 2."

and

"Let's call it a day. We're pooped!"

The fact I have lived to tell this story gives me instant credibility to anyone who ever who complains to me about their job. I simply launch into my "Day at the Sewer Plant Story" and watch them squirm. In case you're wondering, my boss had a bumper crop in his garden that year.

When summer jobs were hard to come by, I would buck hay bales for five cents a bale. After cutting his field and raking the hay with his tractor, the farmer used another attachment which formed tightly strung rectangular bales of hay which usually weighed around fifty pounds and were left in almost straight rows across the field. Young guys like me would squat down, grab the binder twine across the middle of our palms, and in one fluid motion (using the power of our lower body) lift and throw the bales onto a flatbed tractor or into the back of a pickup where another hay hand began stacking them sometimes as high as fifteen feet. As the stack got higher, the work got harder. Hay dust would rain down in your face, stick to back or your sweaty neck and often find its way down your shirt. Some guys wore long sleeved shirts to save their forearms and triceps from getting ripped raw and beet red with scratches, but it was always too hot for me, especially when we unloaded the bales in barns which were well over one hundred degrees. Looking back, I still don't know how my 110-poud self- managed to get fifty-pound hay bales off the ground and fifteen feet in the air. I think it was about the technique I was taught and the long arms of the guy reaching down from the top of the stack to help me. At the end of the day the farmer fed us and paid us in cash. It was the hardest and hottest work I ever did, and I'll always remember what my dad said about working in the hay fields: "It'll make a man out of you."

Another job I'll never forget was working in a turkey house. I still have nightmares about a three-day job I had loading turkeys into cages on those big semi-trailers. If you've ever been driving and seen these long and short houses out in the fields you've probably seen the outside of turkey houses. But, trust me, you never want to see what happens on the inside of these places. The first thing I remember on my first day of work was the smell of ammonia, feces, and the foul odor of too many birds in too small of an area with zero ventilation.

I was instructed to herd several big, white turkeys, from a large area of the turkey house into a smaller, fenced in area as they tried to run for their lives to freedom. Once the turkeys had no room to run away and hide, I would grab them by their feet and turn them upside down, which usually rendered them immobile. With one paralyzed turkey on my hip, I would use my other hand to grab a second one and then hand them to a burly and toothless truck driver who would angrily and with great force throw the turkeys into cages stacked high on his truck.

Apparently some turkeys never got the "you're supposed to go para- lyzed when they turn you upside down" memo and instead found a way to contort their bodies upward, look you straight in the eye only inches from your face and start flogging you with their wings. This was the source of my nightmares because it's really hard to shake from one's memory a turkey staring you down while flapping its wings in your face in a last ditch effort to avoid being handed up to the burly toothless man taking it on a one-way trip to someone's dinner table. About half of the turkeys would crap on the top of my hand the moment I swept their feet out from under them, but if the roles were reversed, I think I would probably have done the same. It took several baths with Irish Spring soap and many days before the smell of the turkey house finally left my body.

One of the last jobs I had before leaving home involved building shelves for a new medical warehouse on the army base about ten miles from my house called Fort Leonard Wood (or as many a boot camp soldier referred to it, "Fort Lost in the Woods"). I have always had the deepest respect for men and women who serve in our military, and while I never enlisted like many of my friends did, I remember feeling proud to have worked as a civilian in support of such heroic and sacrificial people.

In my early years as a pastor, I worked with new or young churches who could not afford to pay me a full-time salary. I firmly believe my upbringing and my Crooked River perseverance allowed me to humble myself and work two, sometimes three jobs while also doing the work of a youth pastor, church planter, and even lead pastor. While serving as a youth pastor in Syracuse, New York, I also sold sporting goods and toys for a major retailer. As a church planter and pastor in the Metro DC area, I worked in book sales and store security, and for a time I even resurfaced clay tennis courts. I did data entry for a pharmaceutical company conducting HIV studies abroad and even had a short stint as a mailman.

While working in the men's and boy's department at a major retail store, I finally got discouraged and began to wonder if I would ever be able to live my dream of being a full-time pastor at church. I had a college degree and had followed a dream to start a new church, but I was spending my days sorting socks and repackaging men's underwear. I had hit rock bottom. The place I worked was right across the street from my townhouse, and there were so many days I thought I was going to get road burn on my nose from hanging my head so low in despair as I walked to and from work.

As I continued languishing in the retail work and wondering if I would ever make myself or anyone else proud of me, I tried to do something which always seemed to lift me up: serve others. I decided to throw a party. My co-workers at the giant retail store were all women, and all but one were immigrants to America. I thought a Fortune 500 retailer like the one I worked for would gladly donate some of their generic soda so I could throw a Christmas party for our department. I'll never forget the store manager telling me they would not support my effort. It was a few weeks before Christmas, and this billion-dollar company wouldn't even spring for a few sodas to help me throw a party. The pennies of profit earned on those bottles were worth more to this business than the basic camaraderie and holiday spirit of the employees whose underpaid labor supported its wealth. For the record, this company treated their employees like crap, and I've never worked for a company who cared less about their employees than this one. But I digress. The lack of donation from my "Bah Humbug" employer did not keep my wife and me from throwing a great Christmas luncheon for all these amazing women, many of whom were, like us, struggling to make the ends meet. After the party my spirits were lifted, and not long after that I was finally able to realize my dream of starting a new church and being paid full-time as its founding pastor.

My work history has been a saga of perseverance. It's been an adventure with as many twists and turns as the Crooked River. There were times I felt like I was paddling upstream and only getting further away from where I wanted to be, and other times I felt I was being swept down the rapids to places only God Himself could have planned for me. Each job has taught me something about myself and something about life I would have otherwise never learned. I also felt the real-life experiences I had in all these different jobs actually made me a better pastor than I would have been had I just landed my first ministry straight out of college. I learned so much about people and their pain and struggles. I learned how to lead others and work together on accomplishing goals as a team. I witnessed how quick a manager could get fired for sexual harassment.

I became a better listener and a better communicator and above all else I learned to show up, work hard and do my best not to quit.

These days I tell young adults who are either in college or about to enter the work force to be patient. I try to communicate how they will likely have to work in places and do things they don't want to do or didn't go to college for before they finally get to do the thing they dreamed about and love to do. I tell them they may even discover the job they thought they wanted and went to college for is not what they thought it would be, or that they may find a new passion in another field. They usually smile politely and nod their heads but inside I suspect they are thinking I'm just another old fart who doesn't know their talent level or how the world works these days. If only they knew I have a mental picture of me standing on top of a pile of human feces with a shovel in my hand and a caption which reads, "You Gotta Go to Work."

CHAPTER NINE:
WHY I NEVER GOT GOOD AT GOLF

But there are three things I've learned about climbing a mountain. First, there's almost always a point when you want to give up. Second, you don't get breathtaking views until you push to the summit. And third, the summit is always just after the point where you want to quit.
-Bob Goff, *Live in Grace, Walk in Love: A 365-Day Journey*, 2019

I've been a pastor in the local church for over thirty years, and during that time I've been asked lots of questions about life, the Bible, God, heaven and how to discern God's will in everyday decisions. Surprisingly, though, the question I've gotten the most over the years has absolutely nothing to do with any of those topics. The question I've gotten the most is, "Do you work full time with the church?" Or, stated in a similar way, "Is this your full-time job or do you do something else, too?" I've always viewed the question as coming from an honest, if also ignorant, place and I try not to be offended or even put off when someone asks the question. I smile and patiently reply, "Yes, this is my full-time job if you don't count my side hustle as an exotic dancer" and then watch the puzzled look on their faces as they contemplate what could possibly fill my schedule between Sundays.

There's always been this tongue-in-cheek joke about how pastors preach on Sundays, do an occasional wedding or funeral, visit sick and dying people at hospitals, and spend the rest of their time playing golf.

For me and most of the pastors I know, the reality is that we work six-day weeks, often have meetings at night, maintain "on call" access at all times, and seldom use our allotted vacation days. Maybe that's why I never got good at golf.

I am not dissing golf or those who play it. I actually love the game and am one of the few people who don't play but still enjoy watching it on TV. There was a brief period in my life when I wanted to learn how to play and even owned some rusty clubs someone had given to me. Because I never had time and, quite frankly, the money to practice, I never got better. In fact, I really sucked. After guys from church who invited me to play saw how bad I sucked, they stopped inviting me to play with them. I had a friend named Landon who also sucked at golf, so we started going and sucking at golf together. We had a lot of fun and neither of us got mad when we hit a bad shot because we always hit bad shots. I remember the last time we played. We were on a local course and I hit a ball off the tee which sliced so hard it ricocheted off a tree and actually ended up behind the tee box. Later on the same hole, Landon, who had somehow managed to position himself in the fairway, hit a yardage marker post and his ball went backwards. We were rolling on the ground laughing and I am quite sure, although I need to check with the PGA, we hold some place in golf history as being the only golfers (not yet on the putting surface) to hit two balls backwards on the same hole. Landon and I authored a new motivational slogan for our golf games that day: "Forward Progress."

Although I had been preaching, doing youth work, and managing other church ministries in the mid-80s, I wasn't officially ordained as a pastor until October 16, 1988. The ceremony took place at my home church, the Crocker Christian Church. The elders at the church, who had been like spiritual fathers to me, read scriptures related to the role of being a pastor. I gave a short message about my commitment to honor and teach the Bible and fulfill the role of a pastor. After my message, there was a formal charge to the ministry, and I knelt on one knee at center stage. All the elders came to where I was kneeling and laid their hands on my head and each one prayed for me. While I appreciated the thoughtful and sincere prayers of these godly men, their prayers were really getting long. The downward pressure of their hands on my head was becoming unbearable, and I thought I might become the first pastor in church history to have to be fitted with a neck brace as a result of their ordination. On that evening in October, in a place where I had given my life to Jesus, been baptized, and was now surrounded by friends and family, I agreed to faithfully serve God and others with my life and to persevere through all obstacles which might come my way. I signed my life away to become a Crooked River Pastor. It was one of the greatest decisions I have ever made.

My Crooked River voyage as a pastor was almost doomed before it even got started. While still enrolled at Ozark Christian College and preparing for ministry, I took a summer internship in New Hampshire. My Crooked River upbringing had caused me to consider doing church work in a place where few people were working, and when a pastor who was serving in New England visited Ozark, shared the need for new churches, and gave the plea for summer interns, I quickly signed up. It was a great summer of learning and I loved the family I stayed with, but when I returned to college for the fall semester I had decided to transfer to a state school at mid-term, get a degree in history and become a teacher. Having spent a summer teaching and hanging out with high school students, I was convinced I could better influence the next generation by having a daily, not just Sunday, presence in their lives which the teaching profession would allow more of than any church ministry I was pursuing at the time. Further, having just gotten outside the box of my small hometown upbringing, I was sure the teaching profession would afford me more opportunities to get back to the East Coast. However, within the first few weeks of the new school year, I learned God had other plans, and He used a new professor, Mark Scott, to literally redirect my life and get me back on the path to becoming a pastor. In his daily lectures, chapel sermons, and the way he lived his life, Professor Scott was mentoring me, even if indirectly, into God's calling for my life. At the same time, as I continued to attend Ozark, I felt God was showing me how becoming a pastor would not limit my opportunities to reach young people but actually expand and increase what I could do with my life to truly make a difference.

After graduating from Ozark, I struggled to launch into church ministry. Throughout my four plus years at Ozark, I had heard whispers of people saying there were way more Christian college graduates looking for church job positions than there were churches with open positions, especially in the niche field of youth ministry which was the funnel most new graduates of Bible college flowed into. I interviewed for open youth ministry positions in Tulsa, Oklahoma, and Springfield, Illinois, but was beaten out in both places by fellow graduates. More whispers haunted me. "What are you going to do with a four-year Bible college degree if you can't get hired by a church?" During this time, I was back to living at home and working as a substitute teacher and janitor at the school I had attended. One day I would sub for the science teacher and the next day I would scrub toilets. I had a strong sense my parents were starting to worry about my vocational future, and things at home started to get tense. On so many nights, I found myself burying my head into my pillow and crying out to God, "I'll do anything you want me to do and I'll go anywhere you want me to go... except New York."

While I continued to struggle with finding my way and figuring out where God wanted me to go, I remained faithful to the things I did know and the things which had gotten me where I was. I stayed close to God through personal Bible study and prayer, listened to and sang along with uplifting and positive music, and kept myself clean of the sins many guys my age indulged in. While attending an adult Bible study and prayer meeting at my home church on a Wednesday night with people much older than I was, we were invited to pray for John and Janice, who were starting not one, but two new churches and asking our church for financial support. I remember thinking, "Here's a couple starting two churches and yet here I am sending out dozens of resumes and begging all these churches to choose me. I bet they could use some help." The only issue, I found out, was they were starting churches in... New York.

As a small-town boy from Missouri, I had always imagined New York as being one big city, but apparently it was also a state. John and Janice were actually starting churches in Upstate New York just north of Syracuse. I contacted the church planting organization they were working with, and before I knew it, I had purchased my first car, a Dodge Aspen, and loaded all my earthly possessions in it for my big move to New York. I'll never forget saying goodbye to my family and driving away on the dirt road. I prayed, "God, everything in this car, including me, is yours. Please be with me on this crazy and scary adventure." I was moving away from the Crooked River, but the Crooked River never moved away from me.

Though I was a very inexperienced driver who had mainly stuck to dirt roads and small-town highways, I was fortunate to be led all the way from Missouri to New York by the leader of the church planting group in Upstate New York, a man whose name was Loyal and his wife Bev. I guess if a person is taking a huge leap of faith into an unknown future there can hardly be a better way to start than following someone named "Loyal." Upon arriving in Clay, New York, I stayed with Loyal and his wife Bev for the first few months of my new adventure and their love and support for me were exactly what I needed to get my feet wet and acclimate myself to my new home. Eventually I began working as a youth minister with John and Janice who had, by now, started churches in the small towns of Phoenix and Parish. The church in Phoenix met in a tiny storefront building, while the church in Parish met in the basement of one of the members. I remember preaching one Easter at the basement church in Parish and almost the entire church had left town to visit relatives or head for warmer weather, leaving just me, the piano player, one or two families, and the family dog who was sleeping under the communion table. I had always thought my first Easter sermon was going to be...let's just say, a little more dynamic and better attended.

Even the combination of these two churches could not afford to pay me a salary or provide any benefits as their youth pastor, so I worked full-time selling sporting goods and toys for Sears at a nearby mall. Back then, I wasn't worried about money; I just loved working for the two new churches and leading the teens in my youth groups who got together on weeknights. John and Janice had become not only my spiritual parents but by best friends. John's world famous chili and sense of humor combined with the love and encouragement I received from him and Janice were the reasons I was able to survive in New York in the early years, and there could not have been two more important people in my life during those days.

I believe in Jesus' teaching if one is proven faithful in small things, he or she can be trusted with bigger things. Within a couple years this principle played out for me, and I was hired as the full-time youth pastor at North Syracuse Christian Church. I had a special place in my heart for teenagers because I remembered my own struggles during that period of my life. As a teen I had experienced the battle to figure out who I was and how to live out my faith in Jesus while surrounded by so many temptations and infected with the desire for shallow acceptance. As a youth pastor, I wanted to guide teens on the journey I had already traveled. Part of accomplishing this task involved getting teens away from their normal surroundings for a week. When I was growing up in the church, we would attend week-long summer conferences held on college campuses called Christ in Youth Conferences. These weeks of focused Bible teaching offered amazing worship services with hundreds of other teens, comedy acts and skits, and great recreational opportunities in the afternoons; these programs were transformational to my spiritual life and I wanted the teens in my youth group to have the same experience.

Every year at the conferences we attended, I would have teens making huge spiritual decisions, including baptism. My friend and fellow youth pastor Mike Bowers from Buffalo, New York, also brought his own youth groups to CIY conferences every year. One year, after a teen he had been investing in for years got baptized, Mike, the teen, and others from his youth group celebrated by doing cannonballs into the water from the side of the pool. I loved this childlike celebration so much I decided to adopt it and do it myself whenever the venue allowed for it, and, at least on one occasion when it didn't. The Bible says the angels in heaven rejoice (I hear "party") over even one person who gives their life to Jesus. I figure if angels are up there doing high fives and back flips, why can't we do cannonballs?

Another place I took my teens so they could escape distractions and focus on their walk with God was a rustic camp near Rochester, New York, called Mountain View Christian Camp. While the facilities and amenities were not comparable in style or comfort to the college campus where we stayed for the Christ in Youth conferences, the impact of the week was often just as great, and sometimes even greater. As the dean of so many weeks of camp at Mountain View, I had a front row seat to watch God do incredible work in the lives of these young people who had gathered from small churches across Upstate New York. The chapel building, which was the hub of so many spiritual transformation moments was outfitted with ugly brown bus seats from the 1950s mingled in with old wooden pews which looked like they were from the 1850s. It's no exaggeration to say miracles took place in the little chapel. I watched so many teens give their lives to Christ there and so many others fall to their knees and worship God. I also witnessed campers donate huge sums of money to missionaries in amounts I found hard to believe. The teens who have attended Mountain View Camp have gone on to be pastors, youth workers, missionaries, Bible translators, teachers, CEOs, leaders in the medical field, nurses, high ranking service men and women, inner city teachers, FEMA instructors, and so much more. Many of them look back to their time at Mountain View not only with warm feelings and fond memories, but as a time when they put a stake in the ground marking their commitment to follow and live for Jesus.

Every day at Mountain View Camp ended with a big and beautiful campfire. As faculty members, we always viewed campfires as a time where we simply let the campers share and shine. Someone with a guitar would lead a song or two to help set the mood, and then it was time for the campers to share anything they wanted about how they were feeling or what they sensed God was doing in their lives. It was also a time where they could say "thanks" or share encouraging words to build up others or even express how they were planning to change when they returned home.

There's something about the beauty and mystery of a campfire on a starlit night far away from one's busy and troubled life which creates a safe and open environment for one to honestly share what is real and important. One of my greatest "campfire moments" involved a beautiful young girl who came to the high school week of camp at which I was serving as the dean. She came carrying a ton of emotional baggage. When her mom dropped her off on Sunday afternoon, she fought back tears and told me she wasn't very confident her daughter would even be able to last the week. I got the feeling the mom was leaving her daughter with us in a last-ditch effort to save her from whatever was causing her such great pain. Throughout the week, I simply prayed for this girl and tried to not treat her differently than anyone else. I didn't even bring up her issues with any other staff members. I wanted to see what God could do with a life when He got someone away from their troubles and their past and put them in an environment where they could experience His love and the authentic acceptance of others who were connecting with God at the same time. And then I just sat back and watched it happen.

I saw her open her Bible and listen to what was being shared. I watched her pray and sing to God. I watched her go belly- first down a soapy and slippery plastic sheet we used during recreation time and smile ear to ear when she swiftly slid to the bottom. I watched her come to the aid of other campers who were sad and dealing with emotional burdens they had brought from their home lives. All week long she was like a sponge soaking up every moment of every day. When we got to the final campfire of the week everything in me was hoping she would find the courage to share what God had done in her life during the week.

The last night of camp can be an emotional experience. I always felt anxious for the teens who would be headed home the next day to face the real world and the challenges waiting for them. I had been to enough of these camps to know many of the teens were going back to really tough situations where their families would not be able to relate to their spiritual experience at camp nor offer any support or encouragement for the decisions they had made during the week. I knew others would quickly find themselves running with the wrong crowd when the new school year began and fall into some of the same temptations they swore off at camp. I knew I would need to keep loving them and be there for them when they fell away and then came back to God again. They were, after all, just like me when I was a teen.

At our last campfire, after we sang a couple songs, I stood before the campers at the center of our circle around the fire and thanked my faculty team and the campers for a great week. I reminded the campers how, in the morning, all of us would drive through the protected gate of the camp and head back to our normal lives, and then I challenged them to stay true to what they had experienced during our time together and to keep the commitments they had made. Then I said something like, "Okay campers, this is our last campfire together. Maybe you've been waiting all week to say something; now it's your turn. It's your time." And then I sat on a wooden plank supported by concrete blocks to watch what would happen.

After several teens had spoken and shared tear-filled hugs, the girl I had been watching transform before my very eyes stood before her peers. She didn't go into a lot of details about the baggage she had brought with her to camp. My memory is she shared a story which involved domestic abuse, depression, and suicidal thoughts. She quickly turned the conversation positive and began detailing how much fun she had and how much she had changed at camp. She thanked a few of her new friends and made them promise they would stay in touch and then she said, "I've been to so many group counseling sessions and seen so many therapists in the past couple of years, and none of them were able to give me what I needed and found this week." Then she paused and everyone knew what she said next would be not only be the last thing she said but maybe the most important. She concluded by saying, "I just wish there was someone who could take all the things I've learned and experienced this week and use it in a way to help people who have gone through what I have...Someone who could, you know, add Jesus to the counseling stuff."

While she was still standing before us and in a God-given moment of inspiration, I pushed the rubber button on my flashlight whose beam could light an entire ballfield and pointed it right at her and announced in voice everyone could hear, "How about you becoming that person?" She dried her tears with the sleeve of her hoodie and shook her head up and down a few times. Nothing else needed to be said. Moments like these and hundreds of others I shared with teens all across Upstate New York at summer conferences, Mountain View Christian Camp, and in the church I served in North Syracuse shaped my life and my walk with Jesus in profound ways I will never forget.

In addition to my responsibilities as a youth pastor I also, on occasion, had the opportunity to deliver the Sunday morning message to the whole church. Every once in a while, after preaching, someone would ask, "When are you going to get your own church?" I never heard this as a question from someone trying to get rid of me, but rather as a confirmation I was growing in my gift of public speaking and leadership which, in the evolution of church leader development, meant (at least to me) I was nearing the time to become the main pastor of a church. For me, the next step would not be to fill a senior pastor vacancy in an existing church but, instead, to try my hand at what was becoming a new and exciting method of church growth called church planting or starting churches from the ground up.

The decision to leave youth ministry and uproot my wife from her large and very close family to attempt something new and unpredictable in a place I had never been (Washington, DC, and its surrounding suburbs) was difficult. I think it was harder for Donna, who had lived in New York her whole life, than it was for me. Less than six years earlier, God had directed me from a small town in Missouri to Upstate New York where I had zero relationships and was clueless about what I was going to do when I got there. To me, this was just another part of the journey, and I trusted there would be great rewards on the other side of obedient faith. Admittedly, the stakes were higher this time. Before, when I had moved, it was just God and me; now I had a wife, and our first daughter, Maressa, was just a toddler. As it turned out, Donna was my biggest cheerleader in the move, and were it not for her commitment to Christ and to me we would never have made the move. I remember before we set out to the DC area looking at each other and saying, "Let's give God ten years of our lives in this new place and see what he does."

Our first few years of our ten-year commitment to the DC area were so difficult we wondered if we were going to make it even two years. We had grossly underestimated the cost of living in the DC area, and the financial support I had garnered from churches and individuals wasn't even close to what we needed. I tried to supplement our income by taking a part-time security job with Costco, but it wasn't enough to stop the bleeding. I ended up taking a full-time job at a Christian Bookstore which provided almost zero time for church planting but did provide for a health insurance plan which allowed us to add our second daughter, Jenna, to our family in 1996. Between my responsibilities as a husband, a father to two young daughters, and a full-time book seller, I still found some time to dream and begin making plans for the new church we wanted to start in Germantown, Maryland, but things were not progressing as I had hoped they would.

I knew I was in the right place for a new church plant because every Sunday when our family headed down to attend services in Rockville we witnessed no one else moving in our apartment complex. We sensed no one was headed to church services but us. Our belief was reinforced by the lack of traffic every Sunday morning on Interstate 270 which is one of the busiest highways in America on Monday through Friday. We also studied the demographics of our county and learned that out of the almost million residents where we lived, less than 20 percent had a church home. Still, we struggled to gain any momentum for our new church. We tried to meet neighbors, a few of which eventually joined our church, but we needed help to launch the church. We needed teammates. During this time, I remember lots of honest conversations between Donna and me about our calling, which almost always ended with a desperate question: "If God is really calling us to do this why isn't He sending anyone to help us?" But because we were both Crooked River people, we refused to give up. We kept crying out for God to help and stayed the course.

After two years of very little church planting but very much praying, God called and sent us Mark and Julie, and their young son, Ben as co-workers. Mark and Julie had also graduated from Ozark Christian College, and Mark came with worship leading and tech skills which were exactly what we needed to launch the new church. Julie, who had grown up as a missionary kid, came with a strong work ethic, a heart for people far from God, and some life experience about starting stuff from scratch. With his music and tech skills, Mark could have written his ticket to serve at a hundred different churches across the country, but God directed him to us. Mark even knew he would, like me, have to work a second job, but he still decided to join our dream for a new church. Together we found time to do a couple of benefit concerts in Missouri and New York to raise start-up costs for the new church and then entered what experts in the church planting world call "The Pregnancy Period" of a new church, which meant we were nine months away from our launch date (first public service). During those nine months we frantically purchased sound equipment, nursery supplies, and even office cubicle partitions to be used to create childcare rooms in the hallways of the movie theater where we were planning our first service. Additionally, we worked on recruiting a few members from the Church of Christ at Manor Woods where our families were attending to serve on our launch team. Everything came down to the wire, but on a Sunday in September in 1997, Christ Church at Germantown was born with over 200 people in attendance.

In the early days of our new church I wanted to set our tone as a church who loved and cared for others in our community, especially those with physical needs. Within a couple months of our successful launch I had already planned for us to travel an hour on a Saturday to serve at the Baltimore Rescue Mission. The mission served as an overnight shelter for men recovering from addictions and economic situations which had caused them to become homeless. They served up a hot and healthy dinner every night along with a safe and comfortable bed. The Mission also had a clothes closet which the men could access, and they brought in professionals who provided free health and dental care along with counseling and vocational advice. For spiritual guidance, the Mission hosted a church service every night which the men were encouraged to attend.

Prior to our new church's trip to the Mission, I had received a list of what they needed as well as brief descriptions of jobs our team of volunteers would perform, but I wasn't sure what kind of response I would get in terms of who would show up to help on a Saturday. I was hoping we would take at least one carload of people and a box of canned or dry food items but, much to my surprise, about 12 people showed up with lots of donations including a truck load of brand new Nike sneakers donated by Mike Jones through his dad, former NBA great Sam Jones. I had to laugh at my lack of faith as our new church volunteer team caravanned its way to one of the toughest neighbors in Baltimore with a truckload of Nike sneakers and two other cars filled with eager volunteers. This was the beginning of several other trips and teams which would serve the men and later a women's division at the Baltimore Rescue Mission. On one trip a member of our church who was a mason led a team in building concrete partitions in the men's shower room for much needed privacy. On another trip a church member who worked for a major plumbing company installed new urinals and toilets free of charge. On one of our service days my good friend Darren and I processed a freshly killed deer through a meat grinder. We were told the work of our hands was to be used later to make venison chili for the men's dinner.

As our new church, Christ's Church at Germantown hit "the terrible twos" we began to hit some tough spots. I had never led a church before, and my inexperience was beginning to show in several places. I made some hasty staff member decisions and didn't develop leaders around me. Before long Mark and Julie, accepted a calling to serve a church back in the Midwest, leaving a gaping hole in our Sunday morning service quality. Over a short amount of time I had successfully whittled the church down to about 75 people sitting in metal chairs in a middle school cafeteria. I didn't know if we were going to survive even though I knew I was in the right place and doing the best I could do with what I had.

God had given me about 100 people whom I loved dearly and wouldn't trade for a church of a thousand, but we were barely hanging on and the thought of having to return to a full time secular job seemed like a worse option than just getting a U-Haul and trying something different someplace else. In yet another desperate act of prayer I asked God, "What do you want me to do now?"

The answer came fairly quickly when I received a call from Mark Wilkinson asking if I wanted to share breakfast with him and his friend Dave. I had known Mark when I was serving in Syracuse and he was a new church planter in Albany. Our church back in North Syracuse had helped the new church in Albany by making phone calls to prospective new church members and by sending adults to their church services to help in the children's areas giving their dedicated workers a much-needed Sunday off so they could attend adult services. I had visited and served the children at the church in Albany and met Mark and his co-worker Brent on several occasions. As we met for breakfast Mark told me he had seen the same new church growth potential demographics for Montgomery County I had seen a few years prior. He shared with me how he and a few other families from Albany were planning to start a church near us. As we talked, I shared with him the condition of our church which had great human resources but nothing financial to offer the church they were planning to start. I shared how it would be great having another church in our area as well as some new friends to hang out with. As we continued the conversation, we began wondering what would happen if, instead of two churches working independently, we could join forces and become one. As we discussed the mutual benefits, we agreed to make it a matter of prayer and then make a decision. My wife, Donna, could see the new life which had been given to me when I returned from what remains today as the greatest breakfast meeting of my life.

Before we could agree to a future partnership with the Albany group, I had to do several in-home conversations with the members of our church to get their input and blessing to try something new. As I shared details of my breakfast meeting with Mark and Dave, I cast a vision for what a new church with a new name and vibe would look like. I shared how the Albany team had families coming down who were seasoned Christians and could fill the gaps we needed, and explained how they were also bringing talented teachers, financial and admin people and a gifted female worship leader along with substantial financial backing from other churches around the country. I painted a picture of how the two groups coming together would create a capacity for quick and dynamic growth and would allow me to serve in areas of my giftedness as opposed to trying to be and do everything. We never took an official vote but if we had, it would have marked the first time in church history an entire church said "yes" to such a major shift in direction.

In the spring of 2001, we celebrated the life and memories of Christ Church at Germantown and gave it a proper burial. Within months, the people from our old church and the families from Albany who had moved down were already becoming friends. At a summer picnic shelter at Black Hill Regional Park with everyone gathered, we announced a spring 2002 launch date and revealed the new church name: Journey's Crossing.

Everything was moving forward for the new church on schedule, and I was filled with joy and a newfound excitement for ministry.

And then 9/11 happened.

CHAPTER TEN:

WHY I NEVER GOT GOOD AT GOLF (THE SECOND PART)

By perseverance the snail reached the ark.
-Charles Spurgeon, *The Salt-Cellars*, 1889

E veryone remembers where they were and what they were doing when the tragic events of September 11, 2001, unfolded. Both of our girls were in school and Donna and I were, surprisingly enough, purchasing a life insurance policy from and agent in our home. I'm not sure why we had the television on, but as the news showed scenes of the Twin Towers crumbling before our eyes, we quickly finished the paperwork, and the agent hurriedly packed his papers in a brief case and left. Within an hour I had received two frantic phone calls on my landline from friends who had survived the explosion at the Pentagon, but due to the volume of cell phone activity were not able to reach their loved ones. Calming my heart rate down, I ensured they were truly out of harm's way and then called their family members to pass along the word they were safe and would eventually make their way home. Later we met our girls at the bus stop, and while holding them tighter than we ever had, we tried to explain to them what had happened. The world changed that day, and I remember whispering a prayer to God saying, "How can I help the many people in our area who will be impacted by this horrific event?"

When 9/11 happened, I was in the midst of a huge vocational transition. I was walking our former church, Christ Church at Germantown, through a period of discontinuity while simultaneously making plans for us to be key members of a new church, Journey's Crossing, scheduled to begin in the spring of 2002. The lead pastor of Journey's Crossing, Mark Wilkinson, had just moved into our area only weeks before 9/11. He and his wife Barbara had been frantically working on painting, hauling possessions, decorating, and the dozens of other projects related to moving into a new house while also doing all the back to school tasks parents have to do. Adding to the craziness of all this was they were doing this for four daughters who were attending three different schools! When I called Mark on the morning of 9/11, he and Barbara were so busy they had not yet heard the news but quickly turned on their televisions to catch up on what had transpired in such a short amount of time. A day or so later, when things had settled down a bit, Mark and I met and determined the spring start date of Journey's Crossing was no longer an option. We needed to start the new church as soon as possible.

As I mentioned earlier, the launching of a new church can often take years of groundwork followed by a nine-month pregnancy period which requires 50-60-hour work weeks, usually resulting in either ulcers or nervous breakdowns for the church planters. Now, we were attempting to launch a church in a month. The reasons were obvious to us. During the days and weeks after 9/11, we saw fear, desire for answers, and spiritual hunger throughout our community. There was a pressing and urgent need for a church to enter the scene and become a "spiritual triage unit" for so many hurting and anxious people. God knew we would be in the situation we found ourselves in and had already lined up so many things which allowed for our accelerated launch. For starters, we already had a core group of people committed to the church, which is usually the hardest and slowest dynamic to develop. We had the core group of about 80 people from Christ Church at Germantown who were ready to go along with about 20 others who had moved down from Albany and were part of Mark's launch team. We were a church of 100 before we even opened our doors, and among the people in this group God made sure we had just the right skills and talents to launch. In this group were talented musicians and vocalists who practiced in my garage to prepare for opening day. We had a rock star admin team to keep us organized and efficient. We had leaders for all our children's ministry needs and people ready to lead mid-week small groups. In short, God had given us not only the capacity to start a church in 30 days but also the means to sustain the sizeable crowd he would bring to us. Other things, like our location for the new church, a creative direct mail campaign, indoor signage, all the supplies we needed to be a portable church, and, crucially, funding for the project all fell into our laps like gifts from a kind father. God's grace and work in our preparations kept showing up all over the place, even as we continued building relationships with the people in our community who were reeling and feeling lost from the terrorist attacks which took place less than 30 miles from their homes.

In the interim between the closing our former church and the founding of the new one, our family decided to go back and attend Sunday services at the Church of Christ at Manor Woods in Rockville where we had attended for a couple years when we first moved to Maryland. We still had friends and acquaintances from the church, including Dave and Peggy Beamer, whose son Todd had been one of the heroes who rushed the cockpit of hijacked United Flight 93, which went down on 9/11 over a field in Somerset County, Pennsylvania. Although there were no survivors of the crash, the bravery of the heroes aboard the flight prevented the hijackers from forcing the plane to their intended target and saved lives on a day which took so many. On the Sunday we attended Manor Woods, Dave bravely shared the pain of their loss but also the hope they had of seeing their son again because of his faith in Christ. Donna and I were deeply moved by Dave's words and after the service I felt compelled to ask Dave if he would be willing to share the same message at our new church on what would be week two of our public services. He graciously agreed.

There's usually a huge drop off in attendance numbers between week one's Grand Opening of a new church and week two. Part of the reason is because out of town guests who are connected to the core group come out in support for one Sunday and do not return, but another reason is that, whether we like to admit it or not, people are drawn to parties and new openings and usually don't have compelling reasons to return. Journey's Crossing debuted with nearly 500 people at our Grand Opening, and while our new guests were there, we invited them to return for week two and hear Dave Beamer share the story of his son Todd's faith and how the family was coping with this loss. A good percentage of those who had attended our first week returned for the second week, and once again Dave spoke clearly and directly about our need for God in times of great pain and loss.

By moving our start- up date and being there for our community, connecting Pentagon workers to their families on 9/11, and inviting Dave Beamer to speak at our church services, God was answering my prayer about how I wanted Him to use me to help others get through the pain of 9/11 but his plan for me was only just beginning.

My new responsibilities at Journey's Crossing included sharing the Sunday morning preaching, working with youth (which I was thrilled to return to) and outreach. Only a few weeks removed from 9/11, churches from across the country who were affiliated with our nondenominational brand began sending thousands of dollars earmarked for 9/11 relief and support. Because we were one of the few churches within our affiliation in the DC area, and because we were new and had been started by a reputable church planting organization called Orchard Group, I suddenly found myself sitting on a pile of money with the only spending stipulation being to use these funds to help those negatively impacted by 9/11.

I started with a call to the lead chaplain at the Pentagon. I asked how we as a church might be able to support his efforts at helping people get through the attack on the Pentagon and all the collateral physical and emotional damage which had occurred. I asked if he was available to drive up to Montgomery County so we could pray for him personally and encourage him in the midst of all he was dealing with at the time. He agreed to take some time from his busy schedule to meet with us, and in advance of his arrival I assembled a team from church who put together several small boxes filled with coffee mugs, candy, small inspirational books, and gift cards from chain restaurants which we would later ask the chaplain to pass along to his co-workers and those who came to his office in need of counseling. I'll never forget the overwhelming sense of emotion I felt as the chaplain told stories of how he had to be the one to walk up to houses, knock on the doors, and deliver the horrible news to family members whose loved ones had been killed in the explosion at the Pentagon. After a time of encouragement and expressions of gratitude, our team circled around the chaplain and prayed for him. We added prayers for all those who had lost loved ones as well as the many people he and his team were seeing everyday who were grieving the loss of co-workers and trying to get back to their normal lives at the Pentagon. Then we all grabbed the donated boxes filled with the goodies and gift cards we had assembled and loaded them in his car. It had been an unforgettable evening.

Another group of people in our area who were dramatically impacted by the events of 9/11 were our county's first responders. Police and firefighters along with ambulance drivers and other emergency response workers logged countless hours in the wake of 9/11. Some of our county's first responders served on location at the Pentagon while others kept vigilant watch throughout the county during the days and weeks of uncertainty and heightened awareness. Our church wanted to honor these men and women who were sacrificing so much and providing such a needed service to our community during this scary, uncertain time.

I made phone calls to all the county firehouses and police departments to determine the actual number of officers, support staff, emergency service drivers, and firefighters and then I went shopping! We decided these amazing community servants were worthy of gift cards to area restaurants in an amount which would cover not only their meals but those of their families as well, who also had to sacrifice time being away from the responders. As I went to the first couple of restaurants and tried to explain to the front door host what I was there to do I found myself being needlessly delayed as people tried to decide who I was and what I was trying to do. To expedite the process, I came up with a short, to the point expression which got me to the right person quickly and effectively: "I'm here to buy $5000.00 worth of gift cards, can you get me your manager?" In a flash I would be sitting down with a manager telling the story of how a new church was helping county first responders by gifting them with free meals. The managers were thrilled with our service and all threw in additional cards as well, which was gracious because many of them during this time were struggling to make money as more and more people were staying home out of fear.

After delivering our gift cards and accompanying notes of appreciation to first responders, we turned our attention to workers in small businesses and transportation driven jobs in Washington, DC, who had suffered financially from the events of 9/11. We had heard how the dramatic decline in air travel was causing huge financial needs among those who earned their living in the transportation business, so on the Saturday after Thanksgiving a group of about ten of us from church met at the Shady Grove Metro Station to head downtown to see how we could help. We decided to break into three teams. One team headed into the heart of the city, another into a small business area negatively impacted in Northern Virginia and a final group to Reagan National Airport. Before we got on the subway, we distributed large envelopes containing multiple blank checks. I distributed the envelopes and gave the following instructions, "We don't have an unlimited supply of money to give out today. Please don't issue any checks for more than $500, and before you write or give out any checks simply ask people how their incomes have been negatively impacted because of 9/11." I added, "Let's bring back some great stories to share with our church and our contributors about how God is working to help those in need through our generosity." We quickly circled up for a prayer asking God to lead our efforts and headed down the Red Line of the DC Metro into the city.

I led the team headed to Reagan National Airport, which on any other year on a long Thanksgiving weekend would have been slammed with passengers coming and going; but on that November day in 2001, it was a ghost town. The airport, now around 40 days after 9/11, was only operating at about 20 percent of its capacity. As an extrovert, I thought it would be easy to just walk up to a few strangers, ask a quick question, write some checks, and then get back on the Metro to Shady Grove to reconnect with the two other teams. Instead, I felt strangely nervous and awkward. As I rehearsed my spiel, I found myself disinclined to engage anyone at all. Thirty minutes passed and I hadn't written a single check. I began to fear the potential shaming I would receive from other teammates who would share life changing stories while I, the Outreach Pastor, returned having not written a single check! I decided I needed to pray. I asked God to show me who needed the most help at the airport, and before I knew it, I was making my way down to Ground Transportation.

Due to the lack of passengers, there were only a few cab drivers at curbside, so I walked down a concrete ramp and found myself in a dimly lit and exhaust-filled parking garage where dozens of cabs were waiting their turn to pick up the scant few passengers assembled curbside at Ground Transportation. I went a few cars into the line and soon wrote my first check. Within minutes, those farther back in line had left their cars and were forming a small line waiting for me to write them a check. Word spread quickly about a white dude in the parking garage giving away money, and the next thing I knew, I was at the center of a scene which resembled a soup or bread line in the former Soviet Union. While the men were patient and I never felt threatened, I was glad I had thought better of bringing my oldest daughter (after I had considered bringing her along earlier that day.) Most of the men I wrote checks to were immigrants from the Middle East, but through their broken English I learned the common story of how many of them worked for cab companies and didn't even own their cars. The lack of travelers at the airport had created such competition for fares that many of these guys were not only not making enough money at the end of their shifts: they were actually losing money!

In the flurry of check writing in the cab dungeon at Reagan National, a gentleman handed me a business card and told me he was the manager of an entire transportation company and had recently laid off twenty workers. On the Monday following our trip into the capital, I called the manager and after a brief conversation I began planning a Christmas party for these twenty individuals and their families. When I shared with our church staff the stories from the airport and my newest adventure for a Christmas party for the transportation company, everyone wanted in on the action. Their help and support for the effort was much needed and truly appreciated. We quickly reserved a location for our Christmas party at a luxurious hotel in Crystal City, a neighborhood of Arlington, Virginia. The church staff helped me put together small baskets of Christmas goodies and we prepared $500 checks for each of the unemployed transportation company workers and their families. As I communicated the details and the plans of the party with the company manager, I sensed he was getting nervous about granting us, a Christian church, direct access to his former employees, many of whom practiced a different religion or none at all. He expressed his concerns to me on a phone conversation by requesting we not do or say anything at the party which referenced Christ or Christianity, or would cause people to feel any sense of responsibility or loyalty to our church because of what we were giving them. We were totally fine with the gag order because our intentions from the very beginning were to simply help those who were struggling with no strings attached and no need to "message" an act of love which spoke for itself. No one was more surprised than I was on the night of the party when the manager went to the podium and after welcoming us and getting everyone's attention said, "We all know the reason we are here tonight. It's because many years ago God sent us the greatest gift of all." The same guy who had told us to be mum about Jesus was now pointing people to him! I remember thinking how it was so much better the employees were hearing it from him than from any of us.

The Christmas party was a magical event. Between meeting new people and eating an amazing smorgasbord of food including a freshly cut meat station and tables filled with decadent desserts, I just soaked up all the laughter and smiles and interactions I witnessed between the workers and their families as well as the workers and our church staff. No one wanted to leave, but as it got late each family received their gifts and checks from our church before heading out the front entrance. Many of those who attended the party later sent thank you letters and emails sharing how we had made a big difference at Christmas for their families during a tough time. On our way home our church staff stopped at the National Mall to check out the decorations and find our State's Christmas tree. Though it was freezing cold my heart had never been warmer. It was the Christmas after 9/11 and it was my best Christmas ever.

Almost four years later, on August 29, 2005, I came face to face with my next outreach opportunity. Hurricane Katrina ravaged the southern Gulf States of Mississippi and Louisiana, and once again our church knew we needed to respond. Within a few days we had already secured our base of activity thanks to a church member who had contacts with people on the ground in Bay St. Louis, Mississippi. A quick communication to our church with a list of needed items produced a trailer full of supplies in a matter of days. We hitched the trailer to our church's 15 passenger van and a team of six of us began the long journey from Maryland to Mississippi. About thirty minutes from our destination, my wife, Donna called and asked me to describe what I was seeing out my window. The entire landscape looked as if it had been bombed. Everything had a grayish, mud-coated appearance, and as we were talking, I commented on a living room sofa wedged high in a tree. The closer we got to the epicenter of the storm, the worse things looked. We arrived at a Baptist church building which was hosting our team and one other church group. We offloaded and unhooked our trailer and then claimed a cot in the auditorium. I could see the water line on the wall inside the church left by the flood waters and it occurred to me the very room we were sleeping in had three feet of standing water in it within the last couple of weeks.

Our daily Hurricane Katrina relief efforts in Bay St. Louis consisted of a quick breakfast followed by a drive into neighborhoods where both sides of the street were lined with pile after pile of gray and soggy personal belongings. It looked very much like we were driving into a war-torn village. Equipped with masks, gloves, and basic tools, we were tasked to remove everything from within the houses and make piles of the stinking and soaked debris along the sides of the road. We had been given permission to enter these houses and execute what was called "mud outs" by the homeowners, some of whom worked shoulder to shoulder with us to clean up the colossal mess. In spite of their overwhelming losses, these folks got out early and often in an effort to clean up and rebuild their lives, and we found them to be thankful, humble, friendly, and resilient people. One homeowner seemed almost giddy as he pointed to a ten-foot tree where, a day earlier, he had removed his jet skis which had been parked by his house before the storm.

One of the saddest tasks I have ever undertaken was the removal of so many permanently damaged and water soaked personal belongings from the houses devastated by Hurricane Katrina. I made trash piles of family pictures, framed artwork, keepsake figurines, nostalgic certificates and letters, valuable sports card collections, books, clothing, toys, photo albums, stereo equipment, and so much more. I tried not to get personally attached to the items I was disposing of but in my mind each mud-cased, unsalvageable possession represented a piece of someone's story which could never be replaced.

Our efforts were part of an important process which allowed insurance adjusters and building experts to assess property damage and the structural quality of the houses. After a few long days of hard and emotionally draining work, our team hitched up our empty trailer and headed back to Maryland, but what we had seen and experienced during those few days in Bay St. Louis would stay with us for a very long time.

About four months later I led a second Hurricane Katrina relief team, this time to New Orleans. Because of its position below sea level, the damage done by the flood waters of Katrina to New Orleans was even more severe than what we had witnessed in Mississippi. The months of standing and stagnant water in homes which had been left vacant and unattended made for a real challenge both to our team and others who had come from all over the country to help. The conditions in New Orleans actually created a health concern among the thousands of volunteers. We kept hearing about a condition called "The Katrina Cough," which apparently had infected volunteers whose lungs were exposed to mold spores as a result of digging through dry debris in the clean-up efforts.

We also heard a story of a young man volunteering with his church who became deathly ill with some sort of viral or bacterial infection which was not responding to treatment. As members of his team retraced the teen's exposure scenarios, it was determined his illness was not related to anything he touched or even breathed in but rather to something he ate. Apparently at one of the "mud out" houses he came upon a Little Debbie Oatmeal Sandwich Cookie sitting on a kitchen counter fully wrapped in its original plastic casing and assumed it belonged to someone on his team who didn't want to eat it. Helping himself, the young man ate the snack cake not knowing it had been soaking in Katrina contaminated flood waters for months and had dried out on the counter. According to the story he made a full recovery, but his misfortune became part of my briefing to remind my team of the potential hazards we were working in while touching and hauling the contents of these flood damaged houses. Almost exactly one year to the date after Hurricane Katrina hit, I led a third and final team back to New Orleans where we still found work to do in places which had not even been touched.

My outreach work related to 9/11 and Katrina still didn't prepare me for an encounter with two of the bravest men I have ever met. It was an unfortunate story which brought our lives together in the week leading up to Thanksgiving in 2009.

In the very early morning hours of October 28, 2009, a Marine sniper team left their base for a 24-hour mission to continue their ongoing effort to take the village of Nowzad in Afghanistan from Taliban forces. The platoon had been active in the area of operation for three weeks and, along with British Marines, had begun to establish their presence despite the resilience of their foes. The mission that day was fairly easy as far as missions go. The sniper team would drive up to a certain vantage point near AP Hill, find positions conducive to long range shots, and then kill any Taliban spotted planting improvised explosive devices such as landmines and car bombs. Just a few days earlier, my nephew Tyler Brown, a member of the same platoon, had been on a similar mission when the truck he was riding in, a Medium Tactical Vehicle Replacement (MTVR) drove over a landmine which battered and disabled their truck. Tyler suffered a concussion in the collision which, as a matter of policy, required him to cease personal involvement in combat missions for five to seven days.

Wanting to stay connected to his fellow sniper team members, Tyler began monitoring radio communications early on the morning of October 28. At around 8 AM, Tyler heard the familiar blast of an IED and hoped it was an accidental occurrence of a Taliban setting off their own explosion, which sometimes happened. But not this time. Cory and Joshua, two young Marines in their mid-twenties looking to get better sights for shooting, had come into the courtyard of an abandoned building and detonated an IED. Josh was on top of the IED, Cory was in front of it, and the results were devastating. Each man sustained life-threatening injuries. Cory suffered muscle tears, burns, shrapnel wounds up and down his entire body, head injuries and a condition called "de-gloving" in which the skin is ripped completely off the underlying tissue of the hand. Joshua's injuries were even more gruesome; he suffered severe shrapnel wounds across the body which would result in the amputation of both legs along with multiple other injuries. Both men were losing blood at such high rates that their life expectancy was at about three hours. The Navy Corpsman traveling with the team, who was also injured by the blast, bandaged up the men and applied tourniquets to slow the bleeding, ultimately saving their lives. The first attempt to get medical help to the men using a heavy armored truck with a Combined Anti-Armor Team CAAT failed due to another encounter with an IED, which disabled the vehicle. After further complications, a second team was able to arrive on site to load and carry the men onto medical trucks. During the rescue mission, one of the men carrying stretchers was hit by another IED inside the courtyard. He ultimately sacrificed his life to save the other men.

Cory and Joshua were quickly rushed by medevac to Camp Bastion in Afghanistan in critical condition. After being stabilized, they were transported to a medical facility in Stuttgart, Germany, and then finally to National Military Medical Center in Bethesda, Maryland. With Tyler still deployed in Afghanistan, I got word via Facebook through his wife Jennifer that Tyler's friends had been severely wounded in combat and could use some encouragement. I connected with Jennifer and offered to make the short drive from my house to Walter Reed Army Hospital to visit my nephew's Marine friends. I invited my good friend Tom to join me for the visit, but neither of us was prepared for what we were about to experience. We casually found our way to the right floor of the hospital and stopped at the nurse's station to ask for directions to Cory and Joshua's rooms. We stopped at Cory's room first. His mom was in the room. I quickly introduced myself as Tyler's uncle and explained how Jennifer had given me his name and room number and asked if I might drop by for a short visit. After I introduced Tom and we got through the awkwardness of a stranger and his friend showing up unannounced at the hospital, everyone settled in, and Cory, who was in obvious pain, shared with us the extent of his injuries including the shrapnel entry wounds which ran up and down one side of his entire body. His injured hand was wrapped in a big "boxing glove" sized bandage, and I could tell he was still traumatized by what had happened to him. Tom and I asked Cory's mom if the family needed a place to celebrate Thanksgiving Dinner, and she assured us they were fine and being cared for very well by those associated with the hospital. We prayed for Cory, and he thanked us for our visit. I left the room with so much respect for Cory and his sacrifice. In my heart I knew he would have a long road to recovery, but he impressed me as a tough dude who would fight through his challenges and overcome any and all obstacles.

After Cory's room we headed over to Joshua's, which was only a few feet away. Once again, I quickly introduced myself as Tyler's uncle which, just like for Cory, brought a quick smile to Joshua's face. Though Joshua's physical loss had been greater than Cory's he wasn't in as much pain as Cory on the day we visited. With no shame he showed us his amputated legs and began talking about sports, especially his love for hockey. Like Cory, I found Joshua to be a smart, tough, and good-looking guy who would find a way to bounce back from his life-altering injuries. I heard a ton of hope in Joshua's voice and felt inspired to have been in the same room with both him and Cory. After we prayed, we said "Goodbye" and began making our way back to the parking garage. As we exited the elevator and walked across the shiny floors of the lobby, I had a sudden, unexpected rush of emotion which almost buckled my knees. I wasn't afraid to cry in Tom's presence. We had shared tears in each other's presence before, but I found myself fighting back tears. I slowed my walking down and took a deep breath in an effort to absorb what I had just experienced. I can't remember if I said anything to Tom or if he even noticed I was having a moment of grief on behalf of our new friends. I had been in the presence of Crooked River Men who bravely fought for our country but now faced uncertain futures. My God-ordained encounter with these two brave Marines is a powerful memory which I will carry with me the rest of my life.

In many ways on the day Tom and I left the hospital, Cory and Joshua's Crooked River Stories were only beginning. They eventually left the hospital and went their separate ways. They logged hundreds of hours of physical therapy and doctor visits. They battled through emotional scars and all the challenges which many other wounded vets before them had endured and they refused to give up hope for a promising future. Eventually, each received a purple heart for their valor. Today Cory runs a successful IT business in Springfield Virginia where he leads almost 50 employees and after scoring the winning goal and receiving a gold medal in Paralympic sled hockey, Joshua started his own business as a motivational speaker and has shared his inspirational Crooked River Story with thousands of others. He was also rewarded with the inaugural Pat Tilman Service Award at the 2014 ESPYs.

Looking back, I'm pretty sure my golf career ended the day when Landon and I hit shots which went backwards. I can't actually remember ever playing golf again. My golf clubs ended up in the dumpster and while I never got good at golf, God made sure I had plenty of exciting opportunities to stay busy and get good at being a pastor. I like to think of it as "Forward Progress."

CHAPTER ELEVEN:

WEDDING BLOOPERS AND CANNONBALLS

"But marriage goes in waves. You've got to be patient. People bail and give up on their marriages way too early. They just don't put the work and effort into it. You've got to suck up your ego a lot of times because that can be a big downfall."
-Anna Benson

"Marriage is our last, best chance to grow up."
-Joseph Barth

"Baptism separates the tire kickers from the car buyers."
-Max Lucado

There are two kinds of people who move to the front of the line of those I distinguish as "Crooked River People." First are the ones who, despite internal strife and external pressures, stay married for decades and do the whole "till death do us part" thing. Marriage is hard, and every anniversary needs to be celebrated. Second are those who get baptized and commit to following Jesus and actually cross the finish line of this life to hear Him say, "Well done, good and faithful servant." If following Jesus was easy, I suppose there would be way more people doing it.

Staying faithful to one's spouse and Savior is the stuff of perseverance. The reason I believe this to be true is because I've seen far too many quitters at both.

In my early days of being a pastor, I received a phone call from someone I had never met asking me to perform a private wedding ceremony at their house. It was the last week in December, and the man on the other end of the line sounded desperate to have someone come and do a New Year's Eve wedding. In our conversation he detailed how he and his soon to be bride had called dozens of churches over the last several weeks and couldn't find a pastor to marry them. As a matter of context, the reason they were having trouble finding someone to marry them on New Year's Eve had less to do with the timing and more to do with the fact that most respectable pastors simply refuse to do these kind of ceremonies without insisting the couple do two or three premarital counseling sessions. Most pastors have such a high value of marriage, and they have seen such carnage from divorces, they simply refuse to get involved in these "drive by" wedding ceremonies.

As the man continued pleading his case for me to perform the ceremony, I got caught up in the romanticism of his plan for a New Year's Eve wedding. I also began to feel a bit of pride about how I could rescue this situation and do something the other stuffy church pastors refused to do to help this poor couple who were simply trying to get married. But, if I'm being honest, the prevailing reason which resulted in me slapping on a suit and tie to do a wedding for people I had never met was that it was a quick way to make a couple hundred bucks and back then I needed the money.

When I arrived at the house I was warmly greeted, and my first observation was how they were hanging all over each other. It was as though they could hardly wait for me to pronounce them "husband and wife" so they could, um, consummate their relationship. It was definitely one of those, "Hey get a room" type of situations. I was starting to feel uncomfortable, but was quickly able to regain my poise and carry out all the elements of a traditional wedding:: statement of purpose, message, wedding vows, the exchanging of rings, scripture reading, prayer, pronouncement of marriage, and nuptial kiss. Setting aside its sudden timing, I did this wedding by the book.

Because it was just the three of us for the ceremony, I served as not only the officiant but also as the best man, ring bearer, flower girl, and photographer, none of which were in my contract. When it was over, the new groom paid me cash money and I wished the new, clingy couple marital bliss. I got in my car to drive home to celebrate the rest of New Year's Eve with my family, but the whole thing felt a little slimy to me, like I had just been involved in a pastoral drug deal.

After I watched the giant ball descend at Times Square to ring in the new year I went to bed. At 1:00 AM my phone rang. It was the new groom. In a quick and loud voice, he asked, "Did you send in the paperwork for my marriage yet?" Half asleep but still recognizing his commanding voice, I answered, "No". My wife began to stir from her sleep, so I got out of bed and moved closer to the bathroom. He continued, "Don't send the paperwork in yet. We were at a church party tonight and I found out some things about her past. I think she just married me for my money." I didn't know what to say or do so I stalled by saying, "Tomorrow is New Year's Day and so I probably wasn't going to mail it in until the following day." He responded in an urgent tone with, "Good, don't send it in. I want you to meet me tomorrow at the grocery store parking lot and bring the paperwork with you." Because I was both sleepy and partially in a state of shock, I agreed to meet this now, angry groom in what was actually an abandoned parking lot on New Year's Day to sort out what had to be the shortest marriage in human history.

My wife thought I was crazy to meet with this guy who was big, intimidating, and even had a first name which invoked fear. I assured her we had a decent life insurance policy on me and that I would not be bringing the marriage paperwork with me so that I could use it as leverage in the event he tried to kill me. The unhappy groom met me at the scheduled time and got into my car at the abandoned lot. I was happy he didn't appear to be armed. I let him vent for a few minutes about how he felt he had been duped into getting married. He shared some uncomfortable things about his sex life and her monthly cycle. Finally, I interrupted by saying, "Listen, I no longer care about what happened between you and your wife and I don't want anything to do with this mess. Here's your

$200 back. I'm washing my hands of this." I went on to tell him I had no idea what I was supposed to do about the paperwork, but I would need to call the county licensing department the next day to find out. I ended the conversation by saying, "As soon as I find out what our options are, I will call you." I could tell he was upset I had not given him the paperwork, and as he got out of my car I was just happy he didn't want to start the New Year off by taking the life of a member of the clergy.

On January 2nd I began making phone calls to try to resolve the "marriage from Hell" I had presided over. My first call was to my friend and senior minister Carl at the church my wife and I had attended prior to starting a new church. I felt confident Carl, who had been in ministry for forty years and performed hundreds of wedding ceremonies, would have encountered this situation before and be able to offer me solid advice to get out of the nightmare I found myself in. As I described what went down over the last couple days and how the disgruntled groom was now asking for the marriage paperwork, I asked Carl, in a hopeful tone, "Have you ever encountered a situation like this before?" Without hesitation he answered, "No." Behind his "matter of fact" response was forty years of the kind of wisdom that prevented him from doing these types of wedding ceremonies. Carl didn't judge me. He quickly offered that the people in the licensing department would know exactly what to do. Still, I hung up the phone in shame.

When I called the county marriage license department, their counsel was clear. The patient woman on the other end of the phone call asked me, "Did they exchange marriage vows?" I responded, "Yes". She continued, "Did you pronounce them husband and wife? I replied, "Yes". And then with a very official sounding voice she proclaimed, "Then they are married." And then she added in a stern voice, "Send us the paperwork." I got off the phone, signed the marriage license, folded it up, put it in an envelope, put a stamp on it, and sent it in. With each of these steps I was finalizing, in my own mind, what I was sure was the shortest marriage in modern day history. If I did the math right, their marriage had lasted less than five hours.

Having learned from my mistakes of performing a wedding ceremony without actually getting to know the couple, I developed a plan for premarital counseling and I was eager to try it out on some friends (Pam and Don) from our townhouse community who wanted me to perform their wedding ceremony. I decided to use the very good book entitled, *His Needs Her Needs* by Willard F. Harley. I set up the counseling sessions in a way to cover one of a woman's needs in marriage and one of a man's needs each week. What could go wrong?

I believe it was in my second session of covering *His Needs Her Needs* with Pam and Don something actually did go wrong. I forget which of Don's needs we were to cover from the book that night, but we never got to it. I do remember the need we were to discuss for Pam. It was trust. Harley maintains one of a woman's basic needs in marriage is trust. Women need to believe in their spouse at a deep level. When the foundation of trust is broken, it's extremely difficult to repair. I had no idea as I knocked on the door of their condo on that fateful night, trust had been broken and the fighting had already started.

Pam and Don were not their normal and welcoming selves. She abruptly answered the door and let me in only to retreat to her bedroom. I made my way to the couch with Don, who was also acting uneasy. Together we awkwardly waited for Pam to return. In retrospect I should have seen I had walked into a bad situation. I should have broken the ice by saying, "Hey, is tonight not good for you guys, let's reschedule." But I wasn't smart enough to make such an offer.

Finally, Pam joined and then stood over us. Glaring at us. I was only guilty because I was a man and was sitting next to the man she now despised. I'm not sure how the conversation started but over the next few minutes I learned that Don, according to Pam, had been flirting with some women at a family gathering. Pam was furious as she recounted the events. When Don offered a partial explanation disguised as an apology, Pam became agitated. She shouted, at least three times, "You're a liar!" And then she did something neither of us expected. She grabbed the book *His Needs Her Needs* off the dining room table and literally "threw the book at us". Don was quickly able to raise his arm to prevent the book from doing permanent damage to his face. Meanwhile, Pam stormed off to the balcony and began smoking a cigarette. Don and I were unharmed but nonetheless stunned. Two thoughts quickly passed through my mind. First, I knew in that moment, nothing in my Bible College training had prepared me for what had just happened. Second, I would now have to make a call to the publisher of *His Needs Her Needs* to ask for a paperback version of the book to be used for future counseling sessions to ensure no one would be mortally injured.

Pam finally settled down. With every ounce of conviction I had, I let them know they had a huge crack in the very foundation of what marriage needed to thrive. I talked about how important trust was and how hard it is to build. I talked about how their ability to work through the trust issues would be a test to see if they should even get married at all. As I got up to leave, I recommended we take a few weeks off from our sessions to allow them to work through the issues they were facing. They humbly agreed with me and then I left them to sort things out.

A few weeks later Pam and Don invited me back. Upon entering their condo, I could see things had changed for the better. I asked them to share with me how they had resolved the trust issue and how they were going to build trust in the future. Over the next few weeks, we finished the book and I performed their wedding ceremony. As their family grew and they moved away I lost touch with them, but at last report they were still happily married.

Benny and Judy, my Crooked River Parents, have been married for 61 years. Like the Crooked River winding north across the Ozark plateau they persevered through things like poverty, the loss of their parents and siblings, raising four kids, teenage rebellion, and so much more. In the midst of it all they have stayed together. I never saw them yell or scream at each other. I never saw them hit or throw things at each other. I never heard them speak unkind words to each other. Instead, I saw them love and support each other. I saw them put the other's needs above their own. I saw them work through problems like a team, and while they never showed much physical affection for each other in front us, I knew by the way they spoke to each other and treated each other they were best friends and deeply in love. The "Golden Years" of their marriage haven't been exactly golden. My dad struggles with COPD and circulation problems in his legs while my mom battles with short term memory loss, the result of a stroke and brain aneurism.

Their retirements and physical challenges have them spending 24 hours a day and seven days a week together and, as you might imagine, they get on each other's nerves sometimes. But the beautiful thing I see when I go to visit them, which isn't nearly enough, is how, after all these years, they still do everything they can to serve the other. I've watched my dad, who in my childhood never set foot in the kitchen, care for my mom by taking on some cooking responsibilities, and my mom continues to clean the house and do the laundry and other household tasks my dad might not have the endurance to perform. My dad patiently and carefully helps my mom put on her compression socks to alleviate her chronic leg cramps, and my mom still finds a way to manage the family finances which dad could never do on his own. Dad also leans on Mom to keep track of all the birthdays of the kids, grandkids, and great grandkids birthdays, and to make sure cards and gifts are sent. Together they are living out the vows they made to each other on Christmas Eve in 1959. When Crooked River People say, "I do" they don't just say it; they mean it, and they do it. Ryan Frederick's words are good here: "Marriage is less about perfection and more about perseverance."

Before he became famous as the founder of *eHarmony,* Neil Clark Warren wrote an excellent book titled *The Triumphant Marriage.* The book content was the result of thousands of hours of surveys and interviews conducted among one hundred successfully married couples. Using the data, Warren drilled down to ten common factors which mark successful marriages. One of those factors is a good old fashioned Crooked River Value: commitment[1]. Warren reported that his research found the desire to dig your heels in and stay together, no matter what,

---

1   The other nine include vision, trust, emotional health, passion/chemistry, communication, conflict resolution, sexual intimacy, community, and spiritual life.

was the strength of the successful marriages they studied. These couples talked about how their refusal to give up on each other, even when things got ugly or hard, was key to their marriage success.

I have used Warren's ten common traits for a successful marriage content in both premarital counseling sessions and in many wedding addresses over the years, and while I believe the other nine factors in his book to be both valid and valuable, to this Crooked River Wedding Officiant, commitment is king.

Along with the many weddings I have performed over the years, I have had the honor and joy of baptizing hundreds of people into Christ for the forgiveness of their sins and spiritual rebirth. There are simply no words to describe the feelings of partnering with God to share the news of how Jesus' death on the cross has paid for all of our sins and how baptism, an act of humble faith, connects us to the reality of His forgiveness. In a wedding ceremony people pledge themselves to each other with words like, "forsaking all others." In baptism, we mark and celebrate the same kind of commitment in our relationship to Christ. And just as most wedding ceremonies are the culmination of a Crooked River Story, baptisms share the same storyline of Crooked River perseverance.

It has always been the practice of the churches I have belonged to and pastored at to baptize people by immersion, and in the early days of leading our faith community, Christ's Church at Germantown, I had the privilege of "dunking" a guy who would become a great friend and eventually help me lead medical mission teams into Nicaragua.

When Dr. Frank and his wife Judy first attended our church, which was held at a local movie theater, they came up to me after a Christmas message and identified themselves as being like the magi who brought gifts to the Christ child. In the message I had made the point of how there were many in our community who were spiritual seekers on a journey to find Jesus. As we talked, Dr. Frank mentioned, in passing, how his brother back in Albany had been praying for him and trying to convince him to read a book. Dr. Frank was struggling to remember the title of the book and could only recall the author's last name and a piece of the book's title.

Dr. Frank said something like, "I think the title has the word 'Christianity' in it and I think the author's last name is Lewis." The combination of someone saying their loved one was praying for them and the fact I knew exactly what book he was referring to got me very excited, and I knew in my heart God was working in Dr. Frank's life. I offered, "I bet he's talking about the book, *Mere Christianity* by C.S. Lewis." Dr. Frank quickly affirmed my assumption. I added, "We actually keep a small library of books in the lobby hallway, right across from the popcorn machine, with some classic and important works we encourage seekers to read. Let's go see if that title is out there."

Dr. Frank took *Mere Christianity* home with him and within a few weeks he brought it back to the movie theater where we continued to hold Sunday services. As he handed me the book, I cautiously asked, "Well, what did you think? Was it helpful?" Frank agreed the book had caused him to consider Christianity on an intellectual basis and then added, "When I come to Jesus, I want to come not just with my head but also with my heart." Once again, God was confirming His work in Dr. Frank's life. His humble admission of wanting to come to Christ with his whole being resulted in my sending him home with another book. The second book was by Max Lucado, one of my favorite authors, who writes from his own heart and, in so doing, has captured the hearts of countless others. I gave Dr. Frank a book entitled, *In the Grip of Grace.*

Over the course of the next few months I had the joy and privilege of getting to know Dr. Frank and Judy better. Judy had an incredible Crooked River Story herself which involved a divorce and raising children on her own. As we talked, Judy reconciled her faith decision to a time in her teens when she gave her life to Christ and now, through helping her husband and by attending and being involved in our church she was rediscovering what it meant to follow Jesus in new and exciting ways. As I shared the story of Jesus with them in their home, I became so excited about the prospect of baptizing Dr. Frank in his own swimming pool when the weather got warmer.

At a church social event Dr. Frank and Judy were huddling around a table with some new friends, and as I walked by, Dr. Frank, always the prankster, staged an impromptu baptism discussion. While looking at his friends, he said in a voice loud enough to be heard by me, "I hear this church practices baptism by full immersion." Dr. Frank had obviously been studying the history of the Christian church to which he was soon to be a fulltime member. I knew this because the words "full body immersion" had never come out of my mouth. Without missing a beat, I responded to Dr. Frank's playful commentary, "Yes, that's true Dr. Frank. And we also hold people under the water in direct proportion to the amount of sin they committed over the course of their lives." The quick-witted doctor shot back, "Will scuba gear be available?"

It wasn't long after the "scuba gear" joke that I baptized Dr. Frank. And in honor of my Youth Minister friend Mike Bowers, we did a celebration cannonball from the side of his pool afterwards. Within weeks, Dr. Frank was serving at our little church. We moved from the movie theater to a middle school cafeteria where he helped set up metal chairs, sound equipment, and run the audio-visual media presentation for our Sunday services. One year, at Easter, I asked him to give a medical description of the physical horror which took place when a person was crucified by the Romans in an attempt to help people understand the great sacrifice of Jesus. After a brilliant and moving presentation, Dr. Frank was quick to remind everyone to not focus on the gore but on the great love of Jesus' sacrifice. Dr. Frank's humility and servant heart also played center stage on his first medical mission trip in Nicaragua. I'll never forget encouraging him to take a break from what had been several hours of caring for dozens of patients and have a plate of food at a huge clinic in Managua. Dr. Frank, in a moment of intensity, said, "Give the food to one of the people waiting in line who need it, I'm going to keep working, I'm fine!"

While backyard swimming pools and indoor swim clubs are great for baptism celebration cannonballs, other baptism venues were simply not made for such occasions. This would be another lesson I had to learn the hard way when Bill wanted to be baptized. By now I was serving in my new role at Journey's Crossing Church, and as the person in charge of finding places for people to be baptized in winter months, I was struggling to find a venue to baptize Bill. He was eager to be baptized and didn't want to wait for warmer weather and a swimming pool baptism. I finally landed a location at a local Baptist Church whose name I cannot give you at this point because I'm not sure if the statute of limitations has expired for what I did there.

The Baptist Church I secured was super friendly and accommodating. They warmed the baptism pool, opened the doors, turned on the lights, and left the small group of us who came to support Bill's baptism with the simple instructions, "Turn out the lights when you are finished and make sure you shut the doors when you leave." They were so trusting of us.

Baptism pools in churches are typically giant, light green colored bathtubs with gradually ascending water levels up a set of stairs and a glass shield on the front which keeps water from spilling over the top, allowing people in the pews to actually see a person being baptized. Bill and I entered the tub from a side room and slowly made our way down the stairs into the deepening and warm waters of the giant tub. I said a few words and then gently lowered Bill backwards into the waters of new life in Christ. Bill was a big guy, but I was able bring him up out of the water to the delight and cheers of those who were sitting on the first row of pews in the church building.

After the baptism, Bill led us up the stairs where I fully intended to simply towel off, change into my dry clothes, turn off the lights, shut the doors and head for home. Suddenly I heard a chant which, to this day, I cannot determine the origin of. Were they actual chants by real people or were they just voices in my head? Regardless, the message was ringing loud and clear in my ear as I was preparing to dry off. The voices repeated and increased in volume: "Cannonball. Cannonball. Cannonball." To this point I had never attempted a cannonball inside a church building's baptistery nor had I heard of anyone ever attempting such a feat, but the chants were calling me to throw caution to the wind, and in one of those "hold my beer moments" I stopped drying off and made my way to the top stair of the sacred baptism bathtub. I lunged my body forward and quickly got into a tuck position and landed a perfect cannonball. I emerged to the satisfying roar of the crowd and like a football player who had just scored a touchdown I raised my arm and pointed my index finger upward. I had done it! I had performed, to the best of my knowledge, the only cannonball into a baptistery in church history.

It wasn't until I had dried off and changed clothes and joined the small group who was waiting for me that I experienced the gravity of my stupidity. Apparently, someone at the church had the audacity to place and ancient Bible on a decorative antique stand right in the middle of the splash zone of my baptism celebration cannonball. The Bible looked to be hundreds of years old. It had the appearance of a Bible which should have been locked under glass in some European museum with a card dating it to the second century. The splash of my cannonball had soaked through the pages, covering a section as big the Minor Prophets, and everyone stood in a circle around me and looked at me as though I had just thrown a baseball through a storefront window at Tiffany's.

As I stood there assessing the damage, I quickly began to sort through my options for fixing what was now a sponge Bible. I thought about driving home and grabbing a hair dryer and drying each page one at a time but quickly reasoned it would take too long. I considered trying to find some dry rags and dabbing the pages but realized this would have easily torn the pages. I thought about just ripping the wet pages out, thinking no one would know the difference, but then realized these were Baptists, not Methodists, and someone would surely discover the missing scriptures. I also considered simply calling the Baptist Church office the following morning and confessing what had happened. I quickly chickened out of this option when I considered having to stand before the Baptist Tribunal and telling just exactly how the Bible had been destroyed. I was running out of time and options when I walked up to the ancient Bible, grabbed the majority of the dry pages which encompassed the New Testament and laid them over the soaked pages. In my mind it was a symbol of how the New Testament fulfilled the Old Testament, but honestly it just seemed like the best option for a bad situation. Occasionally, when I'm out eating or meeting people, I see the pastor of the Baptist church and he always gives me one of those, "I know what you did to our church Bible" smiles.

Bill survived the horror of my hijinks that night and went on to faithfully serve our church in so many needed areas and eventually he even became a member of one of my mission teams to Nicaragua before moving on to join his wife at another church. Sadly, it is probably one of those churches where the pastors don't do cannonballs in the baptistery.

Bill and Frank's baptisms were certainly memorable but there's another baptism I performed which was truly special. David and Tammy had been members of our church for a few years when David's elderly mom came to live with his family. "Momma Blake," as we all came to know her, was a delightful soul and everyone at our church quickly grew fond of her. Her health challenges, not the least of which were lung and breathing issues, limited her involvement in our Sunday Services, but she faithfully attended every week, even if it meant sitting outside the auditorium in the hallway. I got the sense that church for Momma Blake was more about people than listening to preaching. It was more about dressing up and getting out with her family and supporting their faith.

As the months went by, David shared with me how his mom was interested in trusting Christ and being baptized. This was surprising to me because I had just assumed she had done both. I set up a time to go to their house and share an hour-long study I have used over the years to help people know and understand what it means to accept Christ and be baptized. Momma Blake was all ears and it wasn't long before she and I had scheduled her baptism at the swim club our church used for baptisms.

As Momma Blake's health continued to deteriorate, I became more than just a little concerned about immersing her. This fear became even more real when, on the day of her baptism she arrived hooked up to an oxygen tank. I had a quick sidebar conversation with David, and he assured me she would be fine and how she was just a little nervous, which explained why she brought her tank along.

There were other baptisms that day and, to be honest, I can't remember any of them. But I will never forget Momma Blake removing her air hose and carefully walking into the shallow end of the swimming pool with David holding her hand on one side and me on the other. I remember thinking how brave and humble she was, and it made me think about how there were so many people in the world who should and could be baptized, but because of fear or pride find reasons not to be. After I spoke a few words, David and I gently baptized his frail and aging mom into Christ. It was a beautiful moment I will treasure for life.

After her baptism Mamma Blake gave me one of the best hugs I have ever received. She was so happy! David and I helped her out of the pool and while she, for good reasons, did not join in on the celebration cannonball, David and I did one in her honor.

Only a few short months later, Momma Blake passed away and went on to her reward in heaven. The family asked me to lead the memorial service. In the service I used the analogy of how pictures capture the moments of our lives and how Momma Blake had left us with albums full of them. Her family and friends shared many of those "mental" pictures throughout the service as we remembered Momma Blake and said our tearful goodbyes. One of the pictures I shared had come to me a couple days after her baptism. It was actually a physical picture of me, Momma Blake, and David in the pool when she was baptized. When Momma Blake got baptized, she received the same promise everyone else receives when they are baptized. It is the promise of forgiveness of sins and new birth. In the picture of the three of us in the pool, Momma Blake is prayerfully looking down at the water and she is wearing a black T-shirt with bold white letters which read, "Free Upgrade."

Marriage and following Jesus both begin with a verbal commitment followed by a celebration. In a wedding ceremony, couples share vows. In a baptism, people often recite the Great Confession. But perhaps most importantly, the commitment involved in both ordinances remind us of the old but much needed adage for our times, "If you're going to talk the talk, you gotta walk the walk" and as a bonus, "It's not about how you start, but how you finish."

CHAPTER TWELVE:

BROKEN HALOS

Angels come down from the heavens
just to help us on our way.
Come to teach us, then they leave us
and they find some other soul to save.
-Chris Stapleton, "Broken Halos," 2017

Occasionally, I think about the many float trips I took on the Crooked River. I can still envision stringers full of fish, slow eddies, shady banks, moss covered rocks and swift shoals. I also see the people with whom I shared the river and my life. I see my dad wearing a white T-shirt, cut-off jean shorts and his favorite floppy fishing hat running the faded blue Evinrude outboard motor attached to the back of the boat. I see my stout shouldered and curly haired older brother Troy on the front bench seat looking out ahead of the boat for submerged boulders or logs to steer my dad around. I see my younger brother Landis with his "almost white" hair tucked under a blue Bass Pro ball cap and a Skoal Bandit protruding from under his lower lip. We didn't always get along as brothers, but we always seemed to come together when fishing and float trips were involved.

Beyond my family there was another cast of characters who rotated in and out on these day-long float trips. My uncles and cousins came down every year from Chicago and Indiana along with local kin folks, friends, coworkers, coaches, our preacher Brother Mac, and most often my dad's best friend who he called Merf. Each of these Crooked River fishing buddies brought something unique and memorable to those fishing trips, and my life was better for having been in the same boat with so many interesting people. I've never been a big fan of the expression "Everything happens for a reason," but I do believe, when it comes to my life, "Every person has a reason." Looking back on my life, I see how God put several people in the boat of my Crooked River journey to show or teach me lessons I otherwise would have never learned. As messengers from God, each of these people had an angelic presence in my life. Some of their visitations lasted but for a moment while others lasted for years, but all of them taught me something I needed and something I have never forgotten. Let me introduce you to a couple of them.

Cleo of Conway

The expression "Wherever you go, there you are" rang true of me during my first couple of years at Ozark Christian College. Much of the low self-esteem and accompanied depression of my adolescence followed me from my hometown in Crocker, Missouri, to Joplin where I attended college. In the beginning, I found life on a Christian campus to be more accepting and fun than what I had experienced back home, but as guys and girls started coupling up, I eventually found myself, once again, on the outside looking in. The loneliness and depression I had battled in high school started coming back, especially on the weekends. I put on a brave face and tried to do just enough social things to stay under the radar of anyone's concern, but I was struggling. In high school when this happened I would retreat to my room with headphones and listen to sad and depressing love songs, or when I became angry, I would pump up the volume to music from bands like Boston, Journey, REO Speedwagon, and Van Halen, or I would head out to my concrete basketball court and spend hours working on my pure left handed jump shot. Neither of these seemed like viable options in Bible College, so I went another route. I closed myself in my dorm room and buried myself in books and started logging how much time per day I spent studying. I went above and beyond what was required for classwork as I became a 1980s hermit. I had no intention of ever sharing all the new, and mostly useless, information I was gathering. It was a drug I was using to dull my pain.

After a few semesters of hiding, I finally got called out by my friend Greg. Ozark Christian College had forever been, and still remains, a ministry prep school. While I was a student there, classes were only offered Tuesday through Friday. Student preachers and youth pastors would pack up and head to churches in Missouri, Arkansas, Oklahoma, and Kansas on Friday afternoons and return on Sunday night. Monday was considered a study day before classes resumed on Tuesdays. Those of us (mostly underclassmen) who did not have churches where we were serving were encouraged to plug into one of the many local churches or join teams from the college which would drive throughout the Four State Area to serve mostly small, local, and underserved churches. These teams provided churches with a guest speaker who would give the morning sermon, Sunday school teachers for all ages including adults, and song leaders and special music performers.

Many of my friends were joining the teams going out to serve area churches on weekends and returning with stories of how much fun it was to get out and actually share what they were learning in the classroom, but I had zero interest in being involved. I was too busy being depressed and studying so I could forget about how depressed I was. I had successfully avoided all these weekend "do gooders" for almost two years until suddenly, and without warning, my friend Greg casually walked by room while I was studying, poked his head inside the door and announced, "Hey Brown, I just came back from a lunch meeting with a team going to Conway Christian Church this Sunday and I signed you up to teach the adult Sunday school class." I remember feeling angry at first. What right did he or anyone have to sign me up for something I had not agreed to do? I remember absorbing the shock of what had just happened and then walking the entire length of the dorm to Greg's room to get more details. Greg was the kind of guy you could not say "no" to and so, more to save face than to serve anyone at Conway Christian Church, I got updated on my responsibility and started preparing for my assignment.

Conway Christian Church was about 90 minutes from our college campus, so we left early Sunday morning to arrive prior to their Sunday School Hour at 10 AM. Greg and I were joined by a couple, maybe three, girls from the college. The church was without a senior pastor, so Greg would give the morning sermon and the girls would teach a children's Sunday school class and lead the congregation in singing during the worship service. It was a small church of about seventy people, many of whom must have been founding members. We barely got out of the car and into the building before I found myself behind a lectern with about twenty pages of notes teaching the adults a Bible lesson on The Feeding of the Five Thousand from The Gospel of John. It was the first time I had ever taught a formal Bible lesson. My forty plus hours of preparation paid off as I confidently shared a wealth of information and application to the fifteen or so elderly students who sat on one side of the auditorium in wooden pews. I was fairly stuck to my notes that day, but when I did look up at my students, I kept noticing one very old woman who used a magnifying glass when reading her Bible even as she held it close to her face.

Unlike the end of a worship service in small churches where, after the service, the pastor goes to the back of the room and shakes everyone's hand while receiving accolades like "Great sermon, pastor," the ending of a Sunday school class is about as eventful as watching grass grow. I prayed and then people got up out of their pews to stretch their legs and go to the bathroom while waiting for worship service to begin. I folded my lesson notes in half and stuck them in my Bible, wondering how I did and if it even mattered. Greg was already laser focused on his sermon and the girls who had traveled with us had been teaching kids while I was teaching adults which meant I would likely receive zero feedback from my first teaching gig. Then God sent me an angel.

The elderly woman who had been using her magnifying glass was standing in the back of the auditorium. From a distance she had the look of someone who wanted to engage with me but was too shy or too humble to move in my direction. God moved me closer to her, and as He did, I saw why she had to use the magnifying glass: she was cross eyed. As I approached her, she timidly stuck out her frail hand which I quickly took in mine. Holding on to my hand she said, "Thank you so much for teaching our class today. I learned so much." I smiled and asked for her name. She said, "My name is Cleo."

"Cleo of Conway" as I came to remember her was an angel to me that day. In many ways she's the reason I became a pastor. Her simple gratitude that day shocked me out my life of loneliness, sadness, and depression while providing me one of the most important lessons of my life which goes something like this: One of the best things you can do to battle your way through the darkness of depression is to use your God-given talents to serve someone else.

Not long after my first visit to Conway Christian Church, a good friend John, who lived on the same dorm floor with me, was hired to become their pastor. I was happy for John and happy for the church, but most of all I was happy I would be seeing more of an angel named Cleo.

Jim's Day in Court

If you've ever wondered what God is like on a day when he attends a good friend's funeral, check out the account of Jesus' raising of Lazarus from the dead as recorded in Chapter 11 of the Gospel of John. If the Bible is not your thing and you still wonder what God is like in the face of human suffering, let me introduce you to another angel. His name is Jim.

You learn a lot about people during a week-long mission trip. There's something about eating three meals a day together, loving and serving kids in the hot sun, being in someone's personal space while being tossed around in a cramped vehicle and then debriefing the day under a beautiful starlit night which accelerates relational dynamics between people who, before the week began, barely knew each other. It was through such an adventure on the island of St. Vincent and while leading a kids Bible camp I got to know and love Jim and Geri.

Jim and Geri met in Kansas City in 1972 at a Christian home Bible study birthed from the Jesus Movement of the '70s. Their first meeting and early flirtations, which included Geri tracing of the words, "I love you" on Jim's back, ignited sparks and a mutual affection that led to the desire to get married as soon as possible. Geri's parents convinced them to slow things down a bit, and after a one-year courtship they were married at the ripe old age of 19. One year later they celebrated the birth of their first daughter and five years later added a second.

Jim and Geri experienced a typical marriage of mountains and valley. In the beginning they were an army family. Next, Jim tried his hand at politics and lost an election for congress in Tennessee to Al Gore. There were also a few failed business adventures, a gig in newspaper publishing, a handful of written novels, and finally a successful consulting business in Washington DC. Through it all, Jim and Geri remained best friends deeply in love.

I first met Jim and Geri at the grand opening of our church, Journey's Crossing, in October 2001. Jim introduced himself as an author and I read his excellent trilogy and passed his books along to others. Since she had relatives in Missouri, Geri always shared funny anecdotes with me, and together, Jim and Geri always loved teasing me about my "hick" pronunciation of a biblical king. I would always say King Nebuchadnezzar with a long "E" like NebuchadnEEEzer and they would come up to me after sermons and laugh at me saying, "How do you pronounce that king's name?" And, "Is that how they say his name in Missouri?"

A few years into their involvement with our church, Jim and Geri introduced me to Pastor Blake from St. Vincent, whom they had been financially supporting for years. Jim and Geri had always dreamed of taking a team of church people to see Pastor Blake's work and do a Bible camp for kids, which, as I mentioned earlier, was how I grew to know and love them as a couple. Eventually, Jim and Geri opted for a different church but would still pop into a Sunday service at Journey's Crossing every few months, and they remained good friends.

On July 27, 2015, Geri was on her way to the grocery store. She patiently waited for the green light allowing her to turn left onto Shady Grove Road near her home in Derwood, Maryland. Suddenly and without warning, a man in his early 20s who was distraught and angry over being dumped by his girlfriend swerved around cars which were stopped and drove straight through the red light at 55 MPH and struck Geri's car on the front driver's side.

Most of the evidence suggested Geri died instantly from her injuries. The young man who caused the accident was shaken but not injured. Witnesses at the scene reported to police that, after removing himself from his car, the man simply sat on the grass on the shoulder of the road almost as if nothing had happened. He made no effort to assist or learn of Geri's condition. He didn't even call 911 for help. He just sat there as if inconvenienced by the accident. Witnesses reported when they asked if he was OK his only interest was to get a ride to his ex-girlfriend's house who, in fact, had a restraining order against him.

On the morning of Geri's death, Jim was listening to a song on the radio he intended to play on the violin for Geri when he returned home from work. Jim wasn't a great violinist, but Geri always encouraged him to play and was his biggest fan. On his way home from work, Jim called Geri to report he was heading home but he didn't get an answer. Forty-five minutes later, after he arrived home, Geri still hadn't shown up at the house. Jim tried calling a few more times over the next hour before finally calling the police. After a series of confusing phone calls Jim was finally directed to Shady Grove Hospital where, after a long and fearful wait, a hospital chaplain shared with him the horrific news of Geri's death.

I was returning from the Philippines on a mission trip and checking a week's worth of voicemails when I heard the news of Geri's tragic passing. Within hours I was on the phone with Jim grieving the loss of his wife and best friend. I shared with Jim words of comfort from I Thessalonians 4:13-14 which speak of the hope of being reunited with loved ones who have passed away. As we talked, I agreed to speak at Geri's memorial service, and in the days leading up to the event I had dreams in which Geri kept telling me to not to talk so much about her at the service but instead, to point people to Jesus, which is exactly what I tried to do.

Over the next few months Jim and his daughters grieved deeply and learned, via Facebook, more about the man who had taken Geri's life. There were strong indications the man struggled with mental illness. He believed himself to be a prophet of God and had been excommunicated from his parents' church for threatening the pastor. He had been incarcerated at various times for one thing or another and, though active in posting on Facebook after Geri's death, never even mentioned he had been in an accident. Through further investigation they also learned the man suffered from schizophrenia, a psychiatric disorder usually characterized by psychotic behaviors including delusions, hallucinations, withdrawal from reality and disorganized patterns of thinking and speech. It was a condition Jim was all too familiar with, having dealt with it in both his father and brother. Once Jim began to understand the man's condition, thoughts of anger and the desire to hold him accountable became meaningless. Additionally, upon learning of the man's family and social conditions, Jim knew suing him would not be worth the effort or result in any gain, financial or otherwise.

When the date of the trial approached, Jim's daughters, understandably, informed him they could not bear to attend the courtroom to see the man who had taken their mother's life. The entire family struggled with the State of Maryland's liberal and lenient laws which would, in effect, treat their mother's loss as a mere traffic violation resulting in a "slap on the wrist" small fine for a man who shouldn't have been allowed behind the wheel of a car. When Jim called and asked me to accompany him for moral support in the courtroom for the trial, I quickly accepted and hoped Jim's day in court would result in some type of closure or justice. He got neither.

Neither of us knew what to expect as we entered the large courthouse building in downtown Rockville. Jim was there to express value for his bride's life, and I was there to do the same and to support my friend. Two police officers who had attended the accident scene, along with a handful of witnesses, and the State's Attorney joined Jim and me as we waited in a shiny, tile floored hallway outside the courtroom. We weren't there long before the man being tried showed up with his mom and no lawyer. Quickly the State's Attorney took the man down the hallway for a private conversation which probably encouraged him to plead guilty and not try to argue his case or it would go very badly for him. After a few minutes, the attorney returned to us with assurances there wouldn't be any fireworks and then the wooden doors were open, and we made our way into the courtroom where the judge was already sitting and ready to hear the case.

Some of the details from the courtroom that day remain a blur to me. I can't remember much of what happened in the first few minutes of the case. I do remember the judge being kind, considerate, and even compassionate toward Jim and his loss. I remember formal charges being read and a police officer relaying the facts of the crash scene investigation. I remember the accused man staring straight ahead with no expression on his face and no remorse in his heart, and how he gave false testimony which was inconsistent with his statements on the original police record. I remember feeling he was defiantly trying to rid himself of any punishment for his wrongs.

When Jim was finally given permission to speak, he expressed, with a grief stricken voice his personal loss and the incredible pain he and his family had endured and then quickly turned to facts which pointed to how the man had in his previous statements perjured himself. Jim was, at the same time, a grieving husband and a powerful attorney demanding answers and justice. Not once, while Jim was speaking, did the accused man even look Jim's way.

In the end, the reckless and defiant driver mumbled a guilty plea, was fined $2000, and got to keep his driver's license. The State's Attorney chose not to pursue perjury charges and Jim was too exhausted to argue anymore. As we were dismissed by the judge, I watched Jim, still shaken, troubled, and confused by the injustice walk over to the guilty man's mother and embraced her with a warm "I know what your son's condition is like" hug, but due to the language barrier their encounter was without words. From there, Jim went to the front of the courtroom and put his hand on the guilty man's shoulder and spoke a few words to him which Jim, even to this day, does not remember. The man remained unresponsive. And then it was over.

Jim's day in court reminded me of how we live on a broken planet with broken people and how our loved ones sometimes get caught in the crossfire of both. It reminded me that justice isn't always served here on Earth, but it will be served in heaven where Jim will break out the violin and play the song he had rehearsed for Geri. And the angel Jim reminded me of Jesus at the funeral of one of his best friends. Jesus himself was angry at death and the broken planet, confused, conflicted, pulled by emotions in a dozen different directions, and he mourned deeply over the loss of his friend.

It took the loss of my friend Geri, her grieving husband Jim, and a day in court for me to understand the simple and profound words of the shortest verse in the Bible which occurred on the day Jesus attended a good friend's funeral. In John 11:35 we read: "Jesus wept."

In the prologue of this book I mentioned how the two lessons I needed most repeated in my life are God's love for me and to not quit. The day Cleo took my hand and thanked me for teaching Sunday School, I felt a surge of God's love flow into the deepest part of my soul. My day in court with Jim was a reminder that justice here on earth may not happen but we should always pursue it, and how a husband's love for his wife never ends even after they are parted by death.

God teaches his love for us and our need for perseverance in dozens of ways. Sometimes He uses the beauty of creation. He also speaks to us through His word, the Bible. He's been known to speak through circumstances and experiences, and even pain. And then, sometimes, He speaks to us through angels disguised as humans.

CHAPTER THIRTEEN:
THE COURAGE OF KEBEDE

Not only so, but we also glory in our sufferings, because we know
that suffering produces perseverance; perseverance, character; and
character, hope. And hope does not put us to shame, because God's
love has been poured out into our hearts through the Holy Spirit, who
has been given to us.
-Romans 5:3-5

Whenever possible, I like to take a smaller scout team to new countries before leading church members and others on cultural learning and serving opportunities (also known as short term mission trips). It was on such a scouting trip that I, along with our church's Youth Pastor Scott, met up with a guy who shared a story which had to be included in this book.

After a 12-hour direct flight from Dulles International Airport just outside of Washington, DC, to Addis Ababa, Ethiopia, Scott and I were exhausted and dreading the eight-hour car ride on what turned out to be a bumpy livestock littered highway. Passing through customs, we made our way out to the parking lot and were quickly greeted by a short, smiling Ethiopian man wearing a blue and red baseball cap. He introduced himself as Kebede from Food for the Hungry. We loaded our suitcases in a van, and within minutes were in a local coffee shop enjoying an espresso and getting to know our new friend. The experience of flying 12 hours and then driving to the region of Oromo is one I would not wish upon anyone.

About halfway through the journey Scott and I had already decided we would opt for a one-night stay in Addis when we would bring others on future trips. Kebede patiently answered dozens of our questions until we finally arrived at our hotel in the city of Nekemte.

For the next three days, Kebede and a team of welcoming and fun-loving Ethiopians who worked for Food for the Hungry showed us the work being done among those living in extreme poverty. Since our church sponsored nearly fifty children in the surrounding villages, Scott and I received the royal treatment of Ethiopian hospitality from coffee (all day long) to food and warm greetings at schools, civic centers, churches, and people's homes. In one schoolyard Scott and I were completely surrounded by loving school children who wanted nothing more than to shake our hands and receive our greeting. Kebede later told me I was the first white male the children had ever seen. We visited school buildings under construction, irrigated farms, fresh water wells, and even got to pay home visits to our sponsored children. Along the way we could not help but notice the humility and servant heart of our host Kebede. His unassuming and quiet demeanor and the obvious respect he had earned from the Food for the Hungry staff in Digga were but a few of his admirable traits Scott and I observed and discussed while on our whirlwind tour of Digga.

Before we knew it, the week was over and we were packed up in the van headed back to Addis where we would enjoy a tourist day and meet Mehary and Paige, missionaries our church had recently begun supporting, for a cultural meal. About halfway through our return journey from Digga, we stopped at a hotel for lunch. I had discovered Kebede was the same age as I was, and as we exited from the van I remarked about how I was getting too old for these trips and then, after we were seated and waiting for our meal, I asked Kebede about his health. Kebede said he was doing pretty well other than the lingering pain he experienced in his back. When I pressed him about the source of his back pain, he added in the lowest key and most unassuming tone possible, "It comes from the time when I was in prison." The words had barely come out of his mouth before Scott and I asked, almost simultaneously, "What were you in prison for?" And for the next 20 minutes, Kebede shared with us one of the most incredible Crooked River stories I have ever heard.

Kebede Lule was born in 1963 in Debre Markos, Ethiopia. His childhood was full of misery, sickness, and malnutrition, and his father's divorce landed him under the cruel and unloving care of his stepmother. Kebede's earliest childhood memories are of not having friends or playmates, but rather following his stepmother around with an umbrella shielding her from the hot African sun. He remembers being verbally and physically abused, and the manipulative, controlling way his stepmom ruled his dad and his siblings.

At the age of seven, Kebede's dad was reassigned to a new region, and while furniture was being piled in the back of the truck along with the kids, Kebede's older brother secretly removed him and his sister and put them on a public minibus to a city where they were to be reunited with their biological mother. At the time Kebede, had no idea what was happening but later learned his dad had prearranged the whole incident to relieve them from the horrors of their stepmom. Kebede's nightmare had finally come to an end.

After being deprived of emotional, physical, and spiritual nurture during his developmental years, Kebede struggled to adjust to his new environment. He became withdrawn and quiet. He rarely spoke to anyone, and when he did, he spoke so softly people could barely hear him. Feelings of inferiority plagued him as he watched kids his own age excel in academics and physical strength while he lagged behind. He failed an academic achievement test which required him to repeat a grade in school.

The ongoing challenges of Kebede's upbringing and new surroundings intensified in September 1974, when a military coup ousted Emperor Haile Selassie's government in an attempt to form a communist state. In short order, Marxist and Leninist ideology became fashionable and then formidable throughout Ethiopia, and these philosophies were quickly integrated into educational systems and even the Orthodox

Church. As a student in middle school, Kebede's world was, once again, being turned upside down.

Learning the Marxist theory of Dialectical Materialism became mandatory for all middle and high school students. Kebede, who had grown up in the church and whose dad was a former minister, was now questioning the new teachings on evolution presented by his teachers. He began reading his Bible and other religious books, tracts, and magazines which he kept hidden in his room. In a strange way, the teaching he was receiving in school designed to drag him away from God actually drew Kebede closer to God. He started to desire to know God better and to learn more about the kingdom of God. He wanted to know the differences between world religions and, having read in the Bible about a coming day of judgement, Kebede desperately wanted to be right with God before it was too late.

By the time Kebede had reached 15 years of age, socialism and its rigid enforcement had a firm grip on the entire country of Ethiopia. Opposition parties were dealt with in severe ways, including imprisonment and public execution. Civil and political freedoms along with the expressions thereof were not only discouraged but denied altogether. Kebede, still searching for his own faith, found himself teaching Sunday school for small children at an Orthodox Church called St. Mark's. He felt lonely and confused at this time as he contemplated the meaning of his own life and his eternal destiny. He even ventured into the Qur'an but eventually continued reading the Bible since it seemed, to him, like the source book for all other religions. When a Muslim teacher and even his own church leaders fumbled and stumbled to answer his most fundamental question, "How can I be sure I will be in God's presence when I die?" he, once again, felt disillusioned, alone, and sad.

Kebede's spiritual journey continued after his sister shared with him a vision of Jesus she had received. He tried to replicate the experience by fasting and praying, sometimes for a whole day, but never received a vision like his sister had experienced. He remained faithful as a Sunday school teacher and began improving in his academics even as he was forced to learn communist ideology, which came with the promise of recommendation letters essential for continuing education at universities and any kind of vocational skill training opportunities under the current regime. Kebede's future became dependent on learning things he disagreed with and participating in the communist local youth leagues.

In September 1978, through a series of relationships, Kebede was introduced to a small group of Christian students who held Bible studies in secret. Within a few meetings he began finding answers to his questions and not just from the mouths of the student leaders but from the very pages of the Bible. The leaders of the group pointed Kebede to the Gospel of John, in particular the fourteenth chapter, where he read about another man who had questions about eternal life. It was Thomas who asked Jesus how he and the other disciples could find their way to heaven and heard Jesus' reply, "I am the way, the truth, and the life. No one comes to the Father except through me." Kebede had finally gotten his answer and felt as if a huge burden had rolled off his shoulders. He respected how the students and his new friends turned to the Bible for answers to life's questions and how they were trying to live out their faith in difficult times.

The Christians Kebede began to hang out with held their Bible studies in secret places, often small and dimly lit rooms. As Kebede entered these meetings he would see people his own age kneeling and praying to God. They sat on uncomfortable wooden benches and spoke in quiet voices, and when the meetings were over each person left the room, one at a time, at different intervals. When he inquired about the secretive nature of their gatherings the leaders told him how they feared persecution not only from the communist government but from the general public and even the Orthodox churches. They reminded him how Christian practice was viewed with suspicion and how their group meetings could easily be associated with or connected to Western countries, even the CIA in America.

In February 1979, Kebede was attending a church youth meeting at Haimonota Abew at St. Mark's Orthodox Church. During the meeting one of the adult leaders cornered Kebede and asked if the rumors were true that he was part of an underground religious group. In front of his peers, Kebede was challenged to confirm or deny his involvement. Taken by surprise he had been discovered, Kebede openly shared his personal struggle to find answers to his spiritual questions, how the group he had joined were finding answers in the Bible and how he had been growing and finding a peace he had never known. As soon as Kebede finished sharing his feelings, he was unceremoniously excommunicated from his church. He walked down the hallway, exited the building, and never returned.

One month later, Kebede was attending a mandatory local communist youth league meeting. After taking attendance the leader began chanting communist slogans the youth members were required to repeat. Among the slogans were, "Down with imperialism," "Down with the landlords," "Go forward with our communist leaders," and "The revolution is above all." As the leader shouted these phrases, Kebede and his fellow youth members shouted them back while shaking their left hands. One Sunday the leader asked Kebede to the lead others in the chanting, but he replied, "No, I won't lead the chanting." The leader had never encountered such resistance and quickly demanded an explanation for Kebede's defiance. Kebede pulled out his Gideon New Testament and read the following passage from the Epistle of James.

"With the tongue we praise our Lord and Father and with it we curse men who have been made in God's likeness. Out of the same mouth come praise and cursing. My brothers this should not be. Can both fresh water and saltwater flow from the same spring?"

Kebede closed his Bible and pronounced he could no longer praise and live for God and at the same time curse people. Almost immediately a young girl who was present at St. Mark's when Kebede had been excommunicated offered to the communist leaders how Kebede had been meeting secretly with a group of religious followers and been asked to remove himself from the church. After the meeting was dismissed, several of Kebede's friends pleaded with him not to defy the church and the government, but he had already put a stake in the ground. There would be no retreat.

The timing of Kebede's courageous stand is important to note. During this time, the military junta known as the Derg was gaining power throughout Ethiopia. Tens of thousands of youth and political adversaries were executed or thrown into prison and millions of citizens were fleeing the country. The dictator, President Colonel Mengistu Haile Mariam followed in the steps of Mao Zedong of China and Stalin of the USSR by enacting a total cultural revolution and he tried to eliminate expressions of "faith in the unseen Creator." The Ethiopian Orthodox Church along with the Muslim faith made up the majority of the Ethiopian population while Protestant churches, most of which were planted by foreign missionaries, were very few in number and viewed as "anti-communist." The military began eliminating Protestant churches by seizing their buildings and imprisoning pastors and church members. This persecution continued into the early '90s.

At 11 AM on Friday April 27, 1979, a Communist Youth League Chairman accompanied by a policeman arrived at a stationary store where Kebede worked part-time. They greeted Kebede and then told him to return with them to the Regional Police headquarters for a brief enquiry. Kebede locked the store door and followed the men on foot for a mile and a half to the police station. As they arrived, they were greeted by three investigators, two in civilian clothes and an officer in full uniform, the chief investigator, who was a man known for his cruelty. Kebede was instructed to sit down and then the two men who had brought him to the station exited.

The inquiry did not go well for Kebede. The questions and the way they were being asked were meant to confuse and frustrate him. He tried to answer the easiest questions and explain his journey of faith, but the interrogators kept interrupting and shouting at him. One of the officers demanded, "Who preached to you?" "Who is the leader of this group?" and "Who are the other believers in this group?" When the interrogators realized Kebede was only interested in sharing his journey of faith and not giving them the information they wanted, the inquiry abruptly ended and the chief investigator ordered the other two officers to return to Kebede's house and conduct a search of his personal belongings and to collect any evidence which would link him to the group of underground believers. The search took place without any official court order. Kebede was not offered a lawyer or parental protection. There were no legal procedures, no due process. Kebede had no idea his life was spiraling down into a dark hole of communist persecution. He was 17 years old.

When Kebede's mom saw him returning home escorted by two police officers, she ran to his aid. She had witnessed several young boys and girls from the neighborhood who had been forcibly removed from their homes by the police, executed, and then thrown in the streets. She was visibly shaking and began asking all kinds of questions, but was quickly dismissed by an officer's deceitful remark about a "minor inquiry" involving Kebede. The officers tore through the house and gathered all of Kebede's spiritual books, magazines, group pictures with friends, Bible, and stamp collection. The evidence was boxed up and the officers ordered Kebede to return with them to the police station. By 2 PM Kebede had been officially arrested and was put into custody at a small prison compound.

The prison compound was home to thirty prisoners. Kebede's cell was 9 feet by 12 feet in dimension and held him and 14 other prisoners at night. Inmates mostly slept in the sitting position and a single tin can was left by the door for prisoners who had to urinate during the night. Kebede had heard horrible stories about life in these prison compounds and as a result he tried to keep to himself during the day. Kebede's sister brought food to him but he was so traumatized he had lost his appetite. He strategically gave the food she brought to other prisoners, earning their favor and keeping himself safe.

Other members of the Bible study began to be incarcerated along with Kebede and while he desperately wanted to talk to them, the older men in the prison warned him against it, saying that if the investigators saw them speaking they would link their cases and have even more incriminating evidence to use against him. During his imprisonment, some of Kebede's fellow prisoners who were there for religious charges were released. Apparently, for some of the prisoners, all they had to do to be set free was to sign an agreement to not follow the "imported religion of the West." Kebede refused to sign such papers. For him, it was never even a consideration.

Throughout his imprisonment, Kebede stood his ground and refused to implicate any of the Christian leaders from his underground church. The authorities even brought in Kebede's sister, who held a high and respected government position to try to convince Kebede to "rat out" his fellow Christians. Much to her frustration, he refused to say anything which would result in his brothers and sisters in Christ being thrown into prison.

As Kebede languished in prison, he became acquainted with some of his fellow inmates, who included many political prisoners along with common thieves. Kebede noted how they walked with a limp and learned they had been beaten across their legs and on the soles of their feet. Others had dark green sores all over their bodies, the results of having been whipped. The thought of having to endure such torture caused Kebede to pray he would never be exposed to the physical punishment his fellow inmates suffered through, but in a dream, God revealed to Kebede he would, in fact, have to pay a severe price for his faith in Jesus.

On Sunday morning April 29, 1979, prison guards entered the compound and called out the names of four political prisoners. The fifth name they called was Kebede. The prisoners were escorted through a backdoor in the compound and then crammed into a Land Rover for transport. They were driven to an old police training facility about four miles from the prison. The facility was now being used as a torture center for those who opposed the government. Kebede and the other prisoners were ordered to get out of the Land Rover and enter an almost vacant building where, one by one, they would be interrogated and then beaten. Kebede listened with horror at the screams of two prisoners in line ahead of him as he waited his turn and then watched them limp by him, bloodied by their torture. Fear seized him as he contemplated how his five-foot, three-inch, eighty-five-pound body could withstand what he was about to face. God had given Kebede a dream about this day in which He revealed his punishment would not lead to death, but instead to ultimate victory. It was the dream and Kebede's unshakeable faith which carried him down a pale gray hallway as his name was called to face the coming brutality.

Kebede came into a wider space in the building where he saw leather straps suspended from the ceiling over a large table with metal legs. An investigator was sitting in a chair behind a desk looking through Kebede's file folder. He looked up at Kebede with demeaning eyes and briefly recounted the charges against him. In an effort to get Kebede to renounce his faith, the investigator asked Kebede if there was anything different or new he wanted to share which was not in the file. Kebede calmly responded that there was nothing new and nothing to add. The investigator ordered Kebede to remove his boots and socks and to sit on the table. Kebede was then instructed to stand up on the table while his two arms were being tied behind his back with one of the dangling straps. The investigator then kicked the table out from under Kebede's feet while simultaneously draping Kebede's lower body over his shoulder and securing the second strap around Kebede's ankles. Kebede was now suspended horizontally with his face toward the floor like a hammock. The investigator grabbed a thick wooden pole and began striking the soles of Kebede's feet sending a sensation like electrical shock up and down his entire body. The beating continued until he received a blow so severe the wooden pole shattered into pieces. Kebede contorted his body to a position where his face was looking up at the ceiling, at which point the investigator used a new wooden pole to beat him on the back and buttocks, striking Kebede in swift upward strokes. Kebede was also struck in the face by the investigator's pole and fist. As the beating continued, Kebede began bleeding uncontrollably, and while facing upward began to choke on his own blood, which he was forced to swallow.

Kebede remained silent, refusing to even scream through his torture, which only served to enrage the investigator, who intensified the severity of his beating. A second wooden pole was broken over Kebede's defenseless body and blood was flowing like a river and pooling on the concrete floor. After a third round of beating, Kebede struggled to breath and everything went blurry. He started gasping for air and then heard the distant voice of another guard shouting at the investigator, "Stop, he's dying!" Kebede lost consciousness for a brief period as he was untied and carried down the hallway and left lying on the floor near the area where the last two prisoners waited for their names to be called. Kebede came to his senses and immediately vomited the ingested blood but was unable to clear it from his face because his arms had been so severely injured. His eyes, completely swollen shut created a sense of confusion as he collapsed from the loss of blood and the extremity of his injuries. Kebede's beating had been so severe and had taken so long the other prisoners who had yet to be punished were instructed to carry Kebede like a rag doll back to the Land Rover. The beatings for that day were over.

Back at the compound Kebede continued to vomit blood. Some of his inmates who had also been beaten at other times comforted Kebede with warm water compresses, Vaseline cream treatments, and massages in an effort to ward off infection and to nurse him back to health. Kebede's family members were forbidden to see him or offer any help to him for two weeks after the beating had taken place, and during this same time period Kebede received no outside medical help or pain-relieving medication. Gradually, with the help of inmates, Kebede began walking again, but life at the prison compound continued to be a daily struggle. Two months after his beating, Kebede was called, once again, into the Regional Police Headquarters for another round of questioning. The two investigators interrogated Kebede about the names of the leaders of the underground church. Kebede never flinched and gave them nothing beyond his own simple explanation of his journey to faith in Jesus. Losing his patience, one of the investigators got up in Kebede's face and threatened him with, "Are you going to stop following this new faith or not?" Undeterred, Kebede responded by saying, "No, I won't stop following Jesus." Exasperated, an officer at the desk recorded, word for word, what Kebede had spoken and then asked him to sign at the bottom of several papers. When Kebede had finished signing, he returned to the prison compound.

Sadly, Kebede's brother was eventually imprisoned for his faith. Their mother tried, even begged, for her sons be allowed to stay in the same cell, but her request was denied. Other Christians were added to the prison compound. Some were beaten but others were not. During Kebede's stay at the compound seven other Christians were imprisoned with him. There were six guys and one girl. And of the seven, four were high school students.

On July 16, 1979, Kebede and his brother were transferred to Debre Markos Central Prison, home to 3000 prisoners. As prisons go, it was an upgrade from their previous situation and afforded recreational, educational, and skill learning opportunities as well as more sanitary conditions and more freedoms. Still, Kebede and his brother were the only teenagers in the entire facility and as their lives and futures rotted away, they wondered if they would ever see the outside of the prison walls.

Of the 26 prison cells in Debre Markos, three were dedicated as "darkrooms." Prisoners in the darkrooms were there because they were waiting to be executed for their political crimes. These prisoners were allowed only a few hours of fresh air and sunlight in the morning before being forced back into their dark, windowless cells. Over a three-week period after his initial arrival at Debre Markos, Kebede heard the dying screams of more than 20 prisoners who were strangled to death. The sounds of the dying men haunted Kebede's mind and kept him from sleeping. Because of his cell's proximity to the darkrooms, Kebede found it hard to shake free from the real possibility he would be the next prisoner to be executed.

Throughout Kebede's time in prison, efforts were being made by his family to get him released, but Kebede's written and signed statement which read, "I will not give up my faith," continued to be an immoveable obstacle. It had now been 6 months since his initial arrest. He had lost an entire school year and had been tortured physically. Kebede was also suffering from a severe stomach disorder which produced constant acid reflux. His family was growing weary of trying to secure his release in the face of his own stubbornness to renounce his faith. Adding insult to injury, some of his fellow Christian inmates looked down on him and judged him for not rising to their expectations of what a Christian should be. Kebede began to withdraw from others and preferred to spend time alone.

During the seventh month of his imprisonment, Kebede began vomiting blood on a regular basis. He lost so much weight he had to be taken to the prison's first aid clinic. After an IV treatment, he was quickly taken back to his cell where, for three days, he did nothing but lie on his dirty prison cell floor in the fetal position. Two days later, the prison official had no choice but to take him out of the prison to a local hospital. Kebede spent an entire month in the hospital but his stomach pain only grew worse. A Cuban doctor in charge of his care suggested to her superiors that he be sent to Addis Ababa for professional help, but the head medical director refused her recommendation because of Kebede's prisoner status.

While Kebede languished in the hospital facing the real possibility of his death, a new Regional Police Commander took office in Kebede's hometown. This man was a distant relative of Kebede's father. Kebede's older sister pleaded his case, and because the new Commander was also a member of the Regional Revolutionary Supreme Court, there was new hope that Kebede's case could be presented and he could be released from prison. Within two weeks of his new command post, Kebede's relative was presenting his case before the governing body. Kebede's case put the judges in a difficult dilemma because on the one hand, Kebede had not done anything egregious or harmful against the government or society worthy of imprisonment and the torture he had received, but on the other hand, these men also had to play the Communist Party Line, which meant they had to protect the revolution from supposed Western intrusion, including religious practices like those Kebede had been involved with. Complicating matters even more was the fact these ruling members were also members of the Ethiopian Orthodox Church who loved God and believed in the Bible. After much deliberation, a decision was made to release Kebede and his brother; the governing body of men determined their time spent in prison was suitable for anything wrong they had done.

Meanwhile, Kebede's health problems brought him to the brink of death. His family members worried he would die before all the paperwork secured his release. Kebede beat the odds and slowly got better before finally being transferred to his third prison at Addis Ababa Central. Five months later, on June 19, 1980, Kebede's name was called over the loudspeaker in the prison yard and he was instructed to gather his belongings for his release. Kebede had spent a total of 16 grueling months in prison when he walked outside the walls to his freedom, but he had no idea his courage and faith would be tested again.

In September 1980, after a short time staying with a relative in Addis Ababa, Kebede made his way back to his hometown. Having presented the proper release certificate from prison to the officials and leaders at the school, Kebede took a semester makeup test and was promoted to the 11th grade. Kebede also took the fearless step of connecting with other Christians and quickly met up with three people from the underground church. This group quickly grew to twenty. This time, instead of meeting formally in a room, they found it safer to talk about their faith, read the Bible, and pray as they walked from place to place. It was during this time a minister of the underground church taught Kebede and the small group of followers essential Christian doctrines and secretly baptized Kebede and five others.

On March 1, 1981, a town-wide youth meeting was called by the Communist Regional Military Commissariat. The goal of these meetings was to both indoctrinate young Ethiopian students and keep them in line with communist ways. One of the speakers forcefully pointed out the "evils" of Western culture and Western religions. He began shouting and making threats about how his office would be taking serious actions against such "anarchists" and "CIA agents." He walked among the students with his piercing eyes and angry expression and firmly stated, "And I know the names of all of you who are involved in these activities and I know where you live." He finished by adding, "We will be taking revolutionary measures against you soon." Kebede's heart raced as these menacing and intimidating words continued to spew from the Communist leader. Kebede knew the term "revolutionary measures" meant things like, arrest, detain, imprisonment, or even public execution.

The speech that day brought back to Kebede's mind all the trauma and torture he had recently endured. Persecution was rampant throughout his country during this time and Kebede began to have thoughts about leaving his hometown to avoid a return trip to prison or something worse. On the way home from the Communist Youth Rally Kebede reasoned to himself, "There's no hope following Jesus in such a situation anymore. If God wants me to follow him, He must take me out of this country; otherwise I cannot continue to live like this." Heavy with this burden, Kebede went home, fell to his knees and started his "Goodbye" prayer to God. He prayed, "Lord I have lost all of my strength to follow you. Take me out of this country or this is 'Goodbye.'" Immediately he heard a voice in his heart telling him to read Psalm 27 from the Bible. He quickly found his Bible and read these words:

The Lord is my light and my salvation—
    whom shall I fear?
The Lord is the stronghold of my life—
    of whom shall I be afraid?
[2] When the wicked advance against me
    to devour[me,
it is my enemies and my foes
    who will stumble and fall.
[3] Though an army besiege me,
    my heart will not fear;
though war break out against me,
    even then I will be confident.
[4] One thing I ask from the Lord,
    this only do I seek:
that I may dwell in the house of the Lord
    all the days of my life,

to gaze on the beauty of the Lord
and to seek him in his temple.
⁵ For in the day of trouble
he will keep me safe in his dwelling;
he will hide me in the shelter of his sacred tent
and set me high upon a rock.

When he finished reading, it was clear God had spoken. Kebede, in that moment, realized God was greater than the Communist leader who had threatened him just hours before. The Word of God filled Kebede with such joy he began singing and dancing and repeating the words from the Psalm, "Whom shall I fear?" And "Of whom shall I be afraid?"

Kebede's newfound courage and God's protection continued into the summer of 1981 when he and three of his friends went to Addis Ababa and attended a Christian youth leadership training program led by a discipleship group called Intervarsity. Kebede continued to grow in his knowledge and application of scripture. In August 1982, one of the elders of the underground church suggested that Kebede take his place and attend a three-day open-air church conference in the southern part of the country where there was very little, if any, persecution of Christians. Kebede was honored to have received the invitation, and because he was still feeling pressure and stress from his family back home, he packed a bag and left without even telling them where he was going.

After a few days of travel, Kebede finally arrived at the Ethiopian Full Gospel Believers' Church Annual Meeting where he was identified as one of one hundred church representatives from throughout the country. The host church, Shone Full Gospel Believers' Church, was one of the few churches in the country operating without any Communist pressure or interference. Kebede was one of over two thousand Ethiopians who attended the three-day conference, which included singing, preaching, prayers, and classes.

At the end of the final session of the conference one of the worship leaders approached the podium and called Kebede's name and asked him to report to a hut which served as the church office. Upon arrival,

Kebede was greeted by a small group of army and police officers. They asked for Kebede's name, looked at a sheet of paper, and then instructed him to sit on a stone leaned up against the wall of the hut. Within thirty minutes, there were twelve other conference attendees who had joined Kebede inside the hut. Without any explanation the entire group was quickly detained and loaded into two police pickup trucks and taken fifty miles away to the city of Hosaena. Of the thirteen prisoners taken captive, three were siblings of the elders from Shone Church. Four others were from Southern Ethiopia and were members of the organizing committee for the conference. The remaining six, including Kebede, were representatives from other churches throughout the country. Among that group, the oldest was sixty-nine and the youngest, Kebede, was only nineteen. Kebede later learned the Communists had been tipped about the open area meeting dates and location, and rather than creating a huge scene and arrest everyone, they arranged through the conference organizing committee to randomly select thirteen people from the over two thousand people in attendance to arrest. And it just so happened Kebede's name was selected.

The prisoners were treated fairly well their first night in Hosaena, but the next day the harsh interrogations began at the local jail. A week passed with no news of whether the group would be released or remain in the jail. Other Christians who had learned of their arrests brought food and shared prayers and encouraging words to the group. At the end of the second week, Kebede and his fellow prisoners were sent to the central prison of the Sub Region to await their verdicts. The prison in the Sub Region had three cells which were designed to hold a total of sixty prisoners; the military filled each cell with more than one hundred human bodies.

As time passed, Kebede began to lose hope in his release. Christians from all over the country continued to visit him and the other prisoners. They brought food, washed the inmates' clothes and supported Kebede and his friends by meeting their physical and spiritual needs. On March 10, 1983, Kebede was called into the warden's office, where charges for "attending an illegal meeting" were brought up again. Kebede and his friends pleaded their case by arguing the same meetings had been conducted for several years prior to their involvement with no charges or arrests against those who had attended. The warden dismissed Kebede and the others with a promise he would announce his verdict in one week. On Thursday afternoon, March 19, 1983, ten of the thirteen prisoners, including Kebede were released from prison. They served a total of seven months for basically attending a church conference.

Kebede's Crooked River perseverance and faith in Jesus cost Kebede a total of almost two years of his life in prison, where he endured horrific and torturous conditions which, on several occasions, almost cost him his life.

When Kebede had finished telling us his story, my friend and our youth pastor, Scott responded by saying, "We spent all week with you here in Ethiopia and now, on our last day here you're just now telling us this stuff!" We all laughed and then I just looked at Kebede in amazement. An innocent question I had asked about his back pain had led to one of the greatest Crooked River Stories I had ever heard. I felt honored and humbled to be in the presence of someone so full of faith and courage.

CHAPTER FOURTEEN:

WHERE THE RIVER
STRAIGHTENS

*When Heaven is going to give a great responsibility to someone, it first
makes his mind endure suffering. It makes his sinews and bones experience toil, and his body to suffer hunger. It inflicts him with poverty,
and knocks down everything he tries to build. In this way Heaven stim-
ulates the mind, stabilizes his temper, and develops his weak points.*
-Mencius, 300 BC
If anyone is thirsty let him come to me and drink.
-Jesus in John 7:37

In the last book of the Bible, Revelation, the Apostle John receives a
vision of heaven, the New Earth, which awaits the faithful followers
of Jesus. Here's how he describes it:

Then I saw "a new heaven and a new earth," for the first heaven and
the first earth had passed away, and there was no longer any sea. I
saw the Holy City, the New Jerusalem, coming down out of heaven
from God, prepared as a bride beautifully dressed for her husband.
And I heard a loud voice from the throne saying, "Look! God's dwelling place is now among the people, and he will dwell with them. They
will be his people, and God himself will be with them and be their
God. He will wipe every tear from their eyes. There will be no more
death or mourning or crying or pain, for the old order of things has
passed away."

He who was seated on the throne said, "I am making everything new!" Then he said, "Write this down, for these words are trustworthy and true."

He said to me: "It is done. I am the Alpha and the Omega, the Beginning and the End. To the thirsty I will give water without cost from the spring of the water of life. Those who are victorious will inherit all this, and I will be their God and they will be my children. (Revelation 21:1-7)

When describing this place which we typically call "heaven," but which is in fact a new earth, he notes it is a city with a river which runs through it.

Then the angel showed me the river of the water of life, as clear as crystal, flowing from the throne of God and of the Lamb down the middle of the great street of the city. On each side of the river stood the tree of life, bearing twelve crops of fruit, yielding its fruit every month. And the leaves of the tree are for the healing of the nations. (Revelation 22:1-2)

The inhabitants who inherit and live forever in the New City are called in this passage, "those who are victorious." In other translations they are called "overcomers." The Greek word is "nikon," which is linked to the Greek word of victory, Nike. No doubt you have heard of the sports apparel and shoe company Nike which gets its name from this word. The word means, literally, those who have competed or fought and came out victorious. The word drips with images of strength, endurance, sweat, and obstacles overcome. It is a Crooked River word. The point is obvious: heaven will be populated with people who persevered here on earth. Crooked River People from all over the world will drink from the river which is incorporated in the New City and flows right alongside Main Street. Can you picture yourself there? Can you see yourself at the river's edge cupping your hands together for a cool drink of refreshing water?

When my oldest daughter Maressa was old enough to learn how to brush her own teeth, she and I went through this nightly routine in which I would put toothpaste on her toothbrush and then mimic the brushing action she needed to take to ensure a good cleaning. After a satisfactory time of brushing, she would hand her foamy toothbrush to me, which I would then rinse off in the sink and then place back in the holder. For some reason there was never a plastic cup in her bathroom, so more times than not, I would cup my hands together, fill them with water and let her drink from my hands. Because I wanted to teach her how to do this practice, I would encourage her to try it for herself. I can still see her tiny hands forming a cup over the faucet as she filled them with water. The problem was never in the filling of the hands. It was always in the transfer of the water to the mouth. The water would always seep through her fingers, run down her arm, and soak the sleeve of her pink Esmeralda Disney pajamas, necessitating a bedtime wardrobe change.

One night after another unsuccessful "make your own cup with your hands" episode, I was tucking her in to bed, and just before praying together, we started talking about heaven. At a very young age Maressa had an advanced spiritual depth which resulted in conversations even adults would have gladly engaged in. That night, Maressa wanted more details about heaven. I did my best to recall and describe some of the features of heaven from Revelation and then I said, "And there's this beautiful, crystal-clear river which flows right through the city up to the throne of God." I could see the wheels of her imagination turning as I paused and let her take it all in. After a few seconds of silence, she asked, "Can you drink from the river?" I quickly responded, "Of course you can, it is the best water you have ever tasted!" Unexpectedly, her faced changed from wonder to concern and I could see something was troubling her. In a voice you hear just before someone is about to cry, she said, "But what if I don't have a cup to drink the water?" In an instant I knew she was thinking about all her failed attempts at drinking water from her own leaking hands, and in one of my best Dad moments ever, I drew her close to my side and said, "Don't worry honey, Jesus will be right there beside you. He will make a cup with his hands just like I do, and you can drink all the water you want from his hands." In an instant, the thought of drinking water from the cupped hands of Christ changed worry into worship and anxiety into a peaceful night of sleep.

The hope of heaven is hardwired into not only children, but every human soul. The Book of Ecclesiastes says this about God and us: "He has made everything beautiful in its time. He has also set eternity in the human heart." You and I were made for the river of life in the New City, but more importantly we were made for the One who sits on the throne and is the river's source.

Recently I had a vision where I was alone in a boat frantically paddling on the left-hand side to avoid the swift current which wanted to take me directly into the bank and the low-lying trees which would have certainly flipped the boat. With great effort I was able to keep the boat just out of trouble and avoid what could have easily been a drowning type situation. As the current slowed down, I could hear the water lapping underneath the boat. My heart began to slow down, and I placed the wooden paddle across my thighs and began to catch my breath. And then it happened... the river straightened.

I paddled for a few minutes until I came upon a pale gray wooden dock where my in-laws were sitting with their legs dangling in the water. Paul, who had his light blue swim trunks on and was wearing his favorite NY Yankees hat, was laughing and splashing water up on Elnora, who was wearing an orange Syracuse basketball T-shirt and obviously didn't want to get her hair wet. For several minutes I watched them hold hands and look into each other's eyes like lovers do and then paddled on while listening to their laughter fade behind me.

I came upon a fisherman in a boat like mine wearing faded denim overalls. Although he was wearing a wide brimmed straw hat, his thick neck was beet- red from the sun. He cast his line up against a submerged log and waited patiently. His line tightened, his pole bent, and within seconds he had landed a keeper smallmouth bass and added it to his stringer of other fish. He wiped his brow with a red bandana, leaned to the side of the boat and dunked his hands into the clear water and rubbed them together. Then I saw him smile and look up to heaven to thank God for the fish he had just caught. I knew from the time I saw his red neck with tufts of curly white hair sprouting from it and the bib overalls I was watching my dad's old fishing buddy Merf doing the thing he loved most during his life.

About ten minutes later, as I continued paddling down the river, I heard two male voices, and saw a father and his teenaged son on the bank of the river. I watched as the son, followed by his dad, carefully placed his feet on small wooden planks they had previously nailed to a huge sycamore tree. Using the planks like rungs on a ladder, they climbed to a fork about halfway up the tree. The dad then reached for and grabbed a long rope suspended from a sturdy tree limb. He gripped a knotted portion of the rope, leaned back, and then swung out over the open water before releasing the rope and falling feet first into river. He emerged from the water, shook his soaked head like a dog and then shouted up to his son, "Let's see what you got big man!" The son had to use a stick to reach the dangling rope, but his dad had barely cleared the landing area before the son had swung from the rope and landed perfectly in the river. When he resurfaced, he shared a laugh and a high five with his dad, and then they swam back to the bank. I watched them swing and drop into the river two more times as they added some acrobatics to their flights and landings. Just as I was getting ready to paddle away, I recognized the dad from one of my wife's old photo albums. It was her husband Dale. And the boy was her son Shane.

On the other side of the river I heard people laughing, and as I paddled closer, the air was filled with the faint smell of grilled hamburgers and hotdogs. In a pavilion I saw people gathered around picnic tables covered with hamburger and hotdog buns, potato chips, baked beans, ketchup and mustard bottles, and a big watermelon. I saw my dad's mom, whom we grew up calling "Ma," walking a platter of freshly cooked hamburgers from the grill to the picnic table. I saw my mom's mother, Grandma Martin, opening the paper plates and potato chip bags. My Aunt Pat was moving around the pavilion taking pictures of everyone with her Instamatic camera. My Aunt Gladys and Uncle Wayne were sitting under a shade tree guarding a canister of homemade vanilla ice cream. Other distant relatives from both sides of my family were laughing and sharing stories in the shade of the pavilion and around the grill. Some of the men were tossing horseshoes while smaller children were running in a grassy area squirting each other with those big "pump action" water gun rifles. I didn't recognize everyone in this party of what looked to be about fifty people and I would have loved to stay and watch more, but I could tell the current was getting a little faster, which meant I had to keep moving down the river.

Five minutes later I came to a green and freshly cut field with soccer nets on each end. I was drawn to the familiar and beautiful voices I heard speaking Amharic. Handsome young men were sharing the field with beautiful women many of whom were proudly wearing the bright green, yellow, and red striped shirts with a lion on the front representing their homeland of Ethiopia. As they ran and played, I remembered Kebede's stories of how many Christians both young and old had become martyrs for their faith in Jesus during the communist regime in Ethiopia. Because I'm a sports nut, I eased my boat up to a position of midfield and watched the pure joy of people who no longer lived with pain, fear, or the threat of being harmed by evil.

The sun was beginning to drop lower and I knew my float trip was coming to an end. I felt drawn to paddle to an area where a mom and her young, pre-teen son were tossing a football. The boy was strikingly handsome and already athletic in build. His mom was beautiful and the football she threw to her son had some zip on it. I watched the boy run some wide receiver patterns which would have made even professionals take notice. The look of pride on the mother's face with each catch was pure joy for me to watch. I knew who this family was. It was Jessica and Jimmy. I watched them play and then sit down together and drink bottles of red Gatorade. They seemed so happy and free. The evil which had ended their lives on earth was nowhere to be found in the city or by the river that runs through it.

I paddled away from Jessica and Jimmy and within seconds it became clear I was no longer moving or steering the boat. Something or Someone was now serving as the captain. I laid the paddle along the inside of the boat and I tried to take in as much of the scenic beauty and fresh air as I could as I began moving closer to the shore. As I arrived onshore, I heard a sound which would be strange to most ears but not to mine. I heard the sound of gravel scraping the aluminum on the bottom of my boat followed by a softer, sandier scrape along the bottom of my boat. For float fishermen, it is the sound which signals the float trip is over. I stood up on weak legs and stretched my sore back and shoulders and then stepped out of the boat. Before heading further inland, I turned and took one last look at the river I hope to someday enjoy forever.

Acknowledgements (River Guides)

To my siblings Troy, Kristan, and Landis: It wasn't always easy and we weren't always as kind to each other as we should have been but there's no one on earth I would want in the boat going down the Crooked River more than you.

Donna: Thank you for letting me share the tragic story of your life which, still today, brings tears to my eyes. Among my many blessings, sharing my life and love with you is one of the greatest. Thanks for calling me back :)

Maressa: You really should get a "Do Over" for your mission trip. The way you persevered through our time in St. Vincent and continue to navigate the challenges life throws at you means you have Crooked River blood flowing through your veins. Thanks for encouraging me to write my story and for allowing me to share some of yours with my readers.

Jenna: I think you, more than anyone else kept encouraging me to write these stories and to keep going when I felt like quitting. Thanks for using your English Major to help me keep the book clean and for major editing shifts in a couple places which were "game changers".

Victor Thompson: You win the award for "most time spent on Crooked River Stories other than the author" and I am forever grateful.

The train would still be in the station without your hard work. Your gift to me is now a gift to others.

Mark Scott: Your arrival as a professor at Ozark Christian College and your influence on me became a tipping point in my life resulting in most of the stories in this book. Thanks for your countless prayers for me and my ministry over the years

Mike Bowers: Thanks for teaching me how to celebrate baptisms (cannonballs) and for so many life-changing moments on mission fields, CIY conferences, youth retreats, Mountain Christian Camp and so much more. Your friendship was one of the biggest reasons I stayed and thrived in Upstate New York.

Bernard Houlehan: As my high school English teacher you got one more chance to "bleed" red ink on one of my writings and it was SO helpful. Thanks for teaching me the love of writing and reading great books.

Mark Wilkinson: Thanks for believing in me and giving me a chance to work with you and Journey's Crossing. So much of this book is the result of your love for and confidence in me. If I have another book in me there is a chapter featuring your perseverance. I already have a title for the chapter, "Mr. Gasconade".

Scott Velasquez: Thanks for kicking my tail over the last two years by simply asking, "Did you write for your book this week?" Your friendship and encouragement were much needed and truly appreciated.

Journey's Crossing (church staff and members) When Jesus promised he would add brothers and sisters to those who left their own families to follow him and do his work, he must have been thinking about you. Keep paddling on your journey!

Crocker Christian Church: Thank you for bringing me up in the faith and then sending me out to make a difference for Jesus. Without you there are no Crooked River Stories.